Fiona Capp is the author of *Writers Defiled:*
Australian Authors and Intellectuals and three _____ ___ _____, *Surfing,*
Last of the Sane Days and *Musk & Byrne*. Her memoir, *That Oceanic*
Feeling, won the 2004 Nita B Kibble Award for Life Writing. She lives
in Melbourne with her partner and son.

FIONA CAPP

My
Blood's
Country

ALLEN&UNWIN

With kind acknowledgment to HarperCollins Publishers Australia and
ETT Imprint for permission to reproduce lines from Judith Wright's poetry

First published in 2010

Allen & Unwin
83 Alexander Street
Crows Nest NSW 2065
Australia
Phone: (61 2) 8425 0100
Fax: (61 2) 9906 2218
Email: info@allenandunwin.com
Web: www.allenandunwin.com

Cataloguing-in-Publication details are available
from the National Library of Australia
www.librariesaustralia.nla.gov.au

ISBN 978 1 74175 487 2

Set in 12/17 pt Dante by Bookhouse, Sydney
Printed by McPherson's Printing Group

10 9 8 7 6 5 4 3 2 1

CONTENTS

To Meredith McKinney,
Pip Bundred
and Caroline Mitchell

South of my days' circle, part of my blood's country,
rises that tableland, high delicate outline
of bony slopes wincing under the winter,
low trees blue-leaved and olive, out-cropping granite—
clean, lean, hungry country . . .

. . . South of my days' circle
I know it dark against the stars, the high lean country
full of old stories that still go walking in my sleep.

Judith Wright, 'South of My Days'

FOREWORD

Sometimes in life you get lucky. Someone of rare vision and remarkable gifts crosses your path and, in ways that may be apparent only to yourself, they touch your life and change its course. I was seventeen when I first met Judith Wright. Everything that followed from this encounter led me, thirty years later, to the places she loved and dwelt in; the landscapes that made her the singular poet and environmental visionary she became. It was a journey I had been waiting to take ever since I first discovered her poetry as a teenager; a journey not only to actual places but into a psychological and imaginative terrain as real as anything recorded on a map.

As I travelled from New England (in northern New South Wales), where Judith grew up, to Queensland where she lived with her husband, Jack McKinney, and daughter Meredith, and then to her property near Mongarlowe 100 kilometres east of Canberra, where she spent her final decades with her lover, Nugget Coombs, what had once been abstract to me took on solid form. We are all shaped by the places in which we live, as much as our relationships. The smells, the textures, the moods, the contours of these places are part of us in ways Judith understood with exquisite urgency. The urgency of someone who sensed in her bones that something had gone profoundly wrong with our attitude to the earth, long before the term 'conservationist' entered public discourse. She wasn't magically blessed with foresight. Rather, her foresight was borne of her intimate knowledge of the land she loved. During my travels through her blood's country, I began to see how her writing and her view of the world sprang out of this solid ground, this living earth.

From this journey, I bring you back the fragile topsoil of those New England paddocks; the rich, red dirt of Mount Tamborine; the clay and gravel of Mongarlowe. The grit of the poet's landscapes that gave us her pearls.

INTRODUCTION

The last time I saw Judith Wright was on a cloudless afternoon in late summer when she was eighty-two years old. After lunch at the Canberra Botanical Gardens' cafe, we went for a walk in the sunshine. We had not gone far along one of the gravel paths when she stopped pushing her walking frame on wheels and paused to look around the well-tended native gardens.

'I remember when this was just a bare hillside,' she said.

We passed some flowerbeds and she pointed out the bachelor's buttons and white everlastings. When we reached the foot of the hill on which the gardens sit, she urged me to go up and have a look at the waterfall.

'It's too steep for me,' she said. 'I'll wait for you here.'

I hesitated, not wanting to leave her. But she waved me away.

Once at the top, I was conscious of every sound. The thrum of cicadas, snatches of bird song, the water falling. All the things that Judith could no longer hear. After sixty years of progressive hearing loss, she was now—as the medical phrase has it—profoundly deaf.

She told me that if a large dog were to bark in her ear, she would hear a distant howl, like a lone wolf on the horizon. The loss of certain sounds was particularly hard to bear: music, birds singing, frogs croaking, people speaking kindly, children splashing in pools.

When I first arrived at her bed-sit that morning and opened the door, she was sitting facing me but did not look up from her newspaper and only registered my presence when I moved towards her. It had been twelve years since I had last seen her. In that time she had suffered a series of heart attacks and had been in danger of losing her sight. Yet she looked well and little changed, although more frail. The same determined jaw and grim smile; the same matter-of-fact air.

The truth was, though, that much had changed. The poet had put down her pen; the activist had all but retired from the public arena; and she had moved from the light-filled bush house near Mongarlowe which she had designed, to a one room bed-sit in Canberra. Yet there was still pleasure to be had in the small amount of nature on offer in the suburbs—the grass outside her flat, the birds, the few trees, the sky and, when she could 'con' someone into it, as she put it, a visit to the botanical gardens.

As I came down the hill from the waterfall, I saw Judith sitting in the shade further along the path, a slightly hunched yet alert figure in a cloud of white hair. The motionless air and soft afternoon light carried with it intimations of the approaching autumn, a wistful dying fall. We sat side by side in silence. I knew this might be the last time I would spend with her. I tried to dismiss the thought but couldn't help feeling there were things I ought to say. Things too big for casual conversation. I ought to thank her for her poetry, and for the encouragement and kindness she had shown me over the eighteen years I had known her. I ought to tell her how much I admired her. I ought to tell her so many things. But she hardly needed me to remind her of what she had achieved or how many lives she had changed. And if I tried, I was sure it would come out sounding clumsy or too solemn. Too much like a farewell.

Some blue wrens started twittering nearby and I was about to point them out to Judith when I realised that she had already spied them amongst the bushes.

'Beautiful day,' she sighed with real pleasure. 'Perfect.'

I smiled and nodded. There was no point speaking as she wouldn't hear me. I reflected on how relaxed and much less preoccupied she seemed than in the past. Ironically, conversation was easier now that she no longer had to strain to catch what people were saying. There was no need for her to guess or pretend to hear. Whenever I wanted to say something to her, I wrote it down in a large notebook and showed it to her. And she replied in her emphatic, gravelly voice.

It was a very different voice from the one I heard in my head when I first discovered her poetry. I was about twelve years old when, for reasons I am no longer sure of, I took a book from the shelf next to my oldest sister's bed. I think it was the cover that attracted me. I remember it as a photograph of swollen puce storm clouds brooding over a dark landscape. The book was Judith Wright's sixth collection of poetry *Five Senses*, published in 1963, the year I was born. At this time I was very much in the thrall of that potent, nineteenth century Romantic myth of the writer as the heroic, sensitive outsider. Wordsworth, Coleridge, Keats, Tennyson. These were the poets in my pantheon of all time greats, a pantheon gleaned from books around the house and from poems read to me and my brothers and sisters at bedtime by our father who, having studied elocution as a boy, knew how to cast a spell. In my mind, to be great you had to be dead. A few Australian writers scraped into this pantheon but they too belonged to the hazy past. I knew that Judith Wright was a major figure on the Australian literary landscape. Perhaps this is why I assumed she too must be dead.

I looked at the biographical blurb and did a calculation, or perhaps I noticed that she was described in the present tense. Then it registered. Judith Wright was not only a woman and an Australian but she was alive. The whole lofty business of writing felt suddenly much closer to home. The fact that Wright was a living, Australian, woman— as opposed to a dead, European, male—changed everything. I had recently started scribbling poetry myself. The first poem I wrote came to me whole. I say 'came' for that is how it felt, as if it had been delivered from outside. And indeed it had, for it was utterly derivative, melodramatic Tennysonian verse about a knight in shining armour. But it came like a gift and it felt magical. After discovering Judith Wright, I began writing about the lemon-scented gums I could see from my bedroom window and about the world I knew. Knights, maidens, castles were no longer a prerequisite. Even that crucial Romantic concept of inspiration, epitomised by Coleridge's ecstatic poet in 'Kubla Khan' who has 'drunk the milk of Paradise', had now been recast. Much as I longed for it, I could never imagine myself in the state of utter transport described by Coleridge. But I immediately recognised and identified with the title poem of *Five Senses*. I knew that tingling, dizzying feeling of a poem coming on, that sense of connection with forces beyond oneself. In my early twenties I realised that I was not *really* a poet, but I've never forgotten that feeling:

> While I'm in my five senses
> they send me spinning
> all sounds and silences,
> all shape and colour
> as thread for that weaver,
> whose web within me growing
> follows beyond my knowing

some pattern sprung from nothing—
a rhythm that dances
and is not mine.

I don't know how, but I managed to get hold of her address. In my final year at school, I sent her a bundle of my poems. Her reply, the first in a correspondence that was to last almost two decades, arrived a few weeks later.

Dear Fiona Capp,

I think your poems show a lot of promise. I don't as a rule try to criticize or make suggestions, because poetry is a very personal thing, and it is the capacity to write (which you have), not the poems themselves, which is important at your age. The best advice I can give you is the same as I always give—read a lot of poetry, find out how and why it affects you, study language, keep writing. I think one of the best disciplines I know of, for young Australians brought up on a diet of English poetry, is to study Chinese and Japanese poems—if not in the original, which you probably never will be able to, then in the best translations you can get. Their kind of aesthetic, which is a bad word for something important, is much sterner and less sloppy than ours, and it does anyone good to try to pare down words to essentials and to see things clearly.

As for my own 'beginnings in the literary world', I didn't have any, except writing and sending poems to various journals. There were very few literary magazines in the 'forties when I began to publish, and I have never belonged to any literary group (anyway I doubt their value to a writer). Essentially, writing is a solitary job (even if you happen to be doing it in a roomful of editors and reporters).

All good wishes,

Sincerely,

Judith Wright McKinney

Now, when I read the letter I see tactfully worded, cautious encouragement. But as a seventeen year old hungry for a sign that I might have what it took, I saw 'promise' and 'capacity to write' and was quietly elated. Then, by sheer coincidence—although it felt like fate—Judith was invited by my school principal to come and talk to the senior classes. By this stage of her life she was weary of talking about herself and her poetry, but was prepared to speak about what really mattered to her: the plight of Aborigines. And suddenly, there she was, in a grey cashmere dress, having lunch with our small Year 12 Literature class and talking about the confrontation at Noonkanbah Station in Western Australia, between the Yongngora tribe and a giant American mineral exploration company who wanted to drill for oil on one of the Yongngora sacred sites. And then, a few weeks later, she returned as guest speaker at the school speech night. Within a matter of months, the flesh and blood woman behind the poems I had fallen in love with had miraculously materialised and entered my life, first through her letter and, then, through her formidable presence.

After this, we remained in touch through letters and occasional meetings. The early 1980s were a hectic and emotionally intense time for Judith as she was deeply consumed by the Aboriginal Treaty Committee and writing *We Call for a Treaty* (1985) with Nugget Coombs, the quietly charismatic economist, political adviser and advocate for Aborigines, who had been her lover for over ten years. I knew that her husband Jack McKinney—the first great love of her life—had died in 1966 but I did not know about Nugget. I was not the only one. The relationship was kept secret from all but close friends and family. (Although estranged from his wife, Nugget did not want to put her or his family through the pain of divorce.) It strikes me now how little I really knew about her life even though I thought I knew so much. We like to believe that poetry is a baring of the soul, that it gives us direct access to what goes on in the poet's heart. And sometimes, it does. But the heart has many chambers. As Judith said to me during our final meeting in Canberra, 'I keep some things to myself because it is not necessary to tell them. And others, because I'd rather *not* tell them.'

Like any deeply private person who finds herself in the public eye, she cherished her secrets. Even as a young woman Judith thought of herself as 'the cat that walks by itself', after the cat in Kipling's *Just So* story of that name. She rarely referred to her relationship with Nugget in her letters, although she made occasional cryptic confessions, like that to her friend, the British poet and scholar, Martin Robertson:

> [O]ver years past, [I] have had a sort of double-senile love, with a man ten years older than myself . . . I didn't tell you of it for we have had to keep it more or less secret, at first for the sake of his own position which didn't admit of flinging of bonnets over windmills so late in life; and also for the sake of his own children . . . Somehow, however, we have had a great deal of happiness and seen much of each other . . . Love is love, no matter what the problems, and always joyful even in the pain.

I saw Judith as an old woman and therefore beyond sexual relationships, and assumed she lived alone at the poetically named address of 'Edge', Half Moon Wildlife District, Mongarlowe, which was stamped on her writing paper. By our final meeting in the 1990s, however, I knew about Nugget. When I visited her in Canberra that last time, there was a photograph of him beside her bed. She told me she missed him badly. Yet even then, six months after Nugget's death, she did not feel able to speak publicly about their relationship.

Another important thing I didn't realise when I first wrote to her was how many other people were making demands of her, and how fortunate I was that she was such a diligent correspondent. Throughout her life, Judith wrote an average of twelve letters a day. It makes me tired just thinking about how she kept up this pace. The sense of public duty and responsibility that drove her clearly cost her much in time and energy that she might have devoted to her own work. When I re-read her letters to me—especially the ones from the 1980s—I am struck by how blithely I took advantage of her generosity.

In 1985, I sent her three pages of questions about her poetry and activism as part of my honours thesis research on her work. She gave detailed replies to my general questions but, when it came to specific interpretations of her poetry and its impact, she baulked: 'After all, this is your thesis, not mine. Also, it is for you, not me, to say what effect my poems may or may not have had on Australian poetry. I do try not to entangle myself in other people's interpretations and theses. I don't have much time and energy left to do my own work, and have to try at least to keep aloof from what isn't my work. I am sure you will understand this.'

I had, earlier that month, briefly caught up with her at the Canberra Word Festival where she was giving a reading of some of her poems. While there, I met her daughter Meredith, who, when I first introduced myself, thought I was someone she'd met in London, also called Fiona. Over the years, my mind did a curious thing with this case of mistaken identity. For reasons that hardly need analysing, I began to believe that someone had mistaken *me* for Meredith. It was not until twenty years later, when I re-read my letter to Judith (one of the few letters I wrote to her which I copied) that I realised how wrong this memory was. Yet it is all of a piece with the way I, as a young writer, assumed the right to make demands of Judith as my 'literary' mother. I cringe now when I read how I signed off that letter with all those questions: 'I hope I'm not being too demanding of your time and patience!' Of course, I knew that I was.

A year later, when I began working for the *Age* newspaper, I again asked if I could interview her. At first she was reluctant: 'I'm a bit browned off with the *Age*, which has had an article of mine on Aboriginal land use in the N.T. for countless weeks without acknowledgment or return, and hasn't so far as I know reviewed *We Call For A Treaty* either.' Finally, there was something I could do for her. I made inquiries about her article and the review. In her next letter, Judith said she was gradually clearing her desk and agreed to an interview.

Most of the time our letters to each other were about writing, her political activities, and what we were both working on. But, in 1989, she wrote to me asking if I would pass on a letter to Phillip Toyne, head of the Conservation Foundation, which was based in Melbourne. She apologised for being 'so James Bond' but said she had reason to believe that her mail was being intercepted because of her environmental and Aboriginal activism. She knew that I was doing a postgraduate thesis about security surveillance of Australian writers and intellectuals, and understood that I would take her fears seriously. I was glad to be of some use and did as she asked. In her next letter she explained that the secrecy concerned the ALP's uranium mining policy, which she had feared was about to change.

Then, in the early 1990s, our correspondence lapsed. I stopped writing to her and therefore she stopped replying. I'm not sure why this happened. Perhaps because I had started writing a novel and needed to break free of the role of acolyte—which I had always adopted in our correspondence—in order to see myself as a fully fledged writer. After a five year break, I wrote asking if I could use some lines from her poem 'The Surfer' as an epigraph for my first novel *Night Surfing* (1996). In my mind, the poem was the pivot around which the novel revolved. The novel concerns a young woman called Hannah, who drops out of university to learn how to 'walk on water'. While working at a cafe by the sea, she meets Jake, who has demons of his own and dreams of surfing at night. They come from different worlds, but what brings them together is a love affair with the sea.

Judith herself loved body surfing—she first got a taste for it as a girl during family holidays at South West Rocks. Later, when she was living in Queensland, she relished the waves on the Gold Coast, before it became a tourist mecca. 'The Surfer', clearly influenced by the exhilarating word-play of Gerard Manley Hopkins, observes a lone surfer driving his brown, muscular body through 'hollow and coil of green', his free-wheeling joy mirrored by the gulls swooping in the air above him. But the sea can never be the surfer's home. As the sun goes down, the poet urges the surfer to come in before the sea becomes rabid and wolf-like, hungry to devour its prey. Ever since taking up surfing as a teenager, I had been drawn to this poem. For my character Hannah—who is just learning what it means to be wiped-out, and who, wave after wave, finds herself smack up against a wall of fear—the poem is about a showdown between the surfer and the sea. A showdown that only the sea can win. When she tells Jake about the poem, he is sceptical. 'What would a poet know?' he asks.

This question, 'What would a poet know?' reverberates throughout the novel. Looking back, I can see that this same question has reverberated throughout my writing, and that it has been the driving force behind this journey.

One day in 1996 a letter arrived from Judith out of the blue. She reflected on how long it had been since we'd seen each other and, in her typically wry way, said that she'd been having an 'interesting' time. She had spent three months in and out of hospitals after a series of heart attacks and a 'vicious' virus, and had recently become 'embroiled in controversy' after the *Canberra Times* revealed that she and Jack were mentioned in ASIO files kept on writers regarded as communists and communist sympathisers in the 1950s. This came on the heels of allegations about Manning Clark being a Soviet agent. She wondered if I'd be interested in writing something on the fifties, perhaps a portrait of that decade. If so, she could provide me with material and recollections of her experience of the Cold War.

As I was going overseas early the following year, I explained that I couldn't follow up on the ASIO story for the present but would still love to write something about her that would not overlap with the biography that academic and activist, Veronica Brady, was doing. When writing my first book, *Writers Defiled: Security Service Surveillance of Australian Authors and Intellectuals, 1920–1960* (1993), I had not been able to get hold of Judith's security file. In fact, there had not been any record of it existing when I had searched. Clearly, there was more to be said on the subject.

A week or so before I left for Europe, a postcard arrived from Judith. It was a haunting photograph of a line of pine trees receding into a fog called 'Braidwood Morning'. In it, she offered a 'New Year's message of encouragement'. She was 'confined to barracks' in the respite room attached to the Braidwood hospital but felt 'fairly ok'. 'This is really just a goodwill message. What you are doing is important and I hope you will go on with it.' She was referring to her hope that I would write more about the Cold War period. At this time, I had no idea how deep her anxiety about surveillance went. It would be years before I fully understood the story behind this postcard and began to come to grips with the dread these fears inspired.

In the early years of our correspondence she signed off, 'Sincerely, Judith'. Later it was 'Best wishes, Judith'. In the final five years, she signed off, 'Love, Judith'. Although I could not claim to have known her as a close friend, I knew that we had established a relationship of affection and trust. In her last note to me a year before she died, Judith said, 'I understand you are going in for motherhood. I've never regretted it myself and without Meredith I'd have little to face my eighties with. Indeed, I doubt if I'd be here. So best of luck and be happy with it.'

When I think back on that final meeting in Canberra—just a few months before I discovered I was pregnant—there is one thing she said that leaps out at me. We had spent the morning talking about the recently released biography, *South of My Days* (1998). The experience of reading her own biography had clearly unsettled her. Instead of giving her a feeling of satisfaction at all she had achieved, it seemed to have left her wondering where all the time had gone.

'I'm going on eighty-three, Fiona,' she said, staring into the middle distance. 'And the more I think about my life, the more I realise I missed it. I shot past it. "Now" is an extraordinary situation, "now" is neither past nor future and "now" doesn't really exist. There is only one instant, if there is an instant at all. I could never really understand time.'

When she said this, I couldn't believe she really meant it. It seemed more of an intellectual reflection than something felt. I couldn't believe that someone who had done so much with her life could really feel that she had 'missed' the moment. Judith was a poet, after all. Poetry was all about being 'in the moment'. It distilled life to its essence, stripped away all inessentials, all pettiness and distraction, and concentrated the reader's mind in such a way that, for the time you dwelt in a poem, you were more alive and alert to life's beauty, intensity and fragility than at almost any other moment. Poems were like dreams where truths were spoken that could not be uttered in ordinary language.

How could she, who had written so spell-bindingly about time and the way we experience it, say that she had never understood it? The more I ventured into Judith's world, the more her observation troubled me. I knew that she had always been preoccupied with the nature of time. The many stages in our experience of it, from childhood to old age, are reflected in her oeuvre. Quite a number of poems from her early to middle period poignantly capture the child's experience of perpetual present—'nothing is ago, nothing not yet'. The title poem of her first collection *The Moving Image* (1953) traces the shift from the child's understanding of time as infinite yet tangible—'time seemed as many miles as round the world . . . / . . . or a sweet slope of grass edged with the sea'—to the adult's awareness of time as linear and beyond our grasp, only slackening its pace 'when we are / caught deep in sleep, or music, or a lover's face.' When she composed this poem, she was still young enough to be confident that she could come to grips with time and triumph over it. The 'lovelier distance' still lay ahead of her.

With age, this youthful confidence in the power of love and creativity to allow one to fully inhabit the present moment, this excitement about what lies ahead, gave way to a kind of resignation, a sense that the further one goes in life, the more elusive and baffling time becomes. In the 1950s, as she settled into domestic life with Jack and began feeling the pressure to earn a living to support them both, she grew more keenly aware of how easily time could get away from you. *The Generations of Men* (1959)—her fictionalised account of her pastoralist grandparents, May and Albert Wright, which is based on their diaries—imagines Albert, after years of unrelenting, back-breaking work to keep their pastoral property in Queensland viable, stopping to reflect:

> Where had the children gone, whose growth he had once looked forward to. Where had the years vanished of which he had once had such hopes? He had seen no more of his life than if he had been a prisoner locked away from it . . . Would his sons, too, be driven in the whirlwind of destruction, and wake perhaps as he was doing, to ask in the end what had consumed their lives?

From the 1960s onward, vast tracts of her time were consumed by environmental and later, Aboriginal, causes as she tried to undo the 'whirlwind of destruction' that her forebears had set in motion. When her final collection of poetry, *Phantom Dwelling*, was released in 1985, there was no longer a 'lovelier distance' lying ahead of her. Now, more than ever, she wanted to stop analysing experience and time, and simply *be* part of the cosmic scheme. But, much as she longed for this unmediated oneness with the universe, she knew that 'human eyes impose a human pattern', illusory as it might be, and that this inescapably separates us from the rest of creation and makes us conscious of the passage of time. On a more personal note, these poems capture how, as one ages, the present silts up with memories from the past. In the late poem 'Dust', drought has 'stopped the song of the river'—the traditional metaphor for time; and her beloved swimming hole—an emblem of the present moment—has almost dried up. Time's current has become so sluggish that past and present merge.

It wasn't until ten years after my final conversation with Judith that I began to understand what she meant, what she *felt*, when she said that she had 'missed' her life. 'Where is the life we have lost in living?' T.S. Eliot asked. Becoming a mother had brought this home to me in a way that nothing else in my experience had. One minute I was cradling a chubby-faced baby in my arms and trying to juggle motherhood and writing and making a living, and then, in what seemed like no time, my son was nine years old and too big for me to pick up. This had happened even though I said to myself, almost every day, never forget these moments, drink him in as he is right now. Hold fast to this day.

At the same time, I clung to the belief that I would learn, as I got older, how to better inhabit the moment. I was encouraged by what I was discovering about Judith's interest in Buddhism and Taoist thought, and her own practice of meditation at her bush property, Edge. She would spend hours on end studying a patch of ground and the life teeming on it, or would sit by the river that ran past her property and observe the small, moment-by-moment changes in the water, the trees, the sky. One way of looking at meditation, says writer Jon Kabat-Zinn, is to view thinking as a waterfall, a continuous cascade. To cultivate what Buddhists call 'mindfulness'—detached awareness of our mental processes—we have to go beyond or behind our thinking, much in the way that you might find a vantage point in a cave behind a waterfall. 'We still see and hear the water, but we are out of the torrent.' This explanation of meditation would have been meaningful to Judith, especially as she floated in her waterhole with the sound of water endlessly tumbling over the rocky ledges at either end.

Almost every day Judith went for walks through her property; walks she described in her letters as 'ecstatic'. She used this word, I think, with full knowledge of what the Greeks call *ekstasis*, the indescribable joy that comes of 'stepping outside' ordinary experience and losing oneself in the moment. In her ever-evolving relationship with the land, she was learning how to dwell in it without imposing herself on it. To accept it for what it was, to see it for what it was, to love it for what it was. She even gave up trying to cultivate a garden, that beguiling mirage of perfection and control. Meditating, Buddhists say, is not a matter of self-improvement or striving of any kind, but of learning how to be fully present.

How then to reconcile this wise acceptance, this rich experience of the moment, with her remarks to me during our final meeting? Was this inevitably how everyone felt towards the end of their life? That for all the extraordinary experiences you packed into it and all the meditating you did upon it, you couldn't help feeling that life had slipped through your fingers?

All that sunny, late summer day in the botanical gardens I had been wanting to ask Judith her thoughts on death. Perhaps she would have something to say that would help make sense of these contradictions.

But I didn't want to put a cloud over our remaining time together. Nor did I want to be presumptuous. She might live for another ten years, I might die tomorrow. Yet I knew that she had spent more time contemplating death (in her poems) than most of us are willing to do, and I wondered what she had learned, and how her feelings about this ultimate deadline might have changed.

Apart from the usual intimations of her own mortality experienced in childhood, death first touched her and irrevocably changed her world when Judith was twelve years old. The only glimpses we have of her immediate reaction to her mother's death come from her very first attempts at poetry. These poems, written between the ages of about eight and thirteen, are contained in two black leather exercise books surrounded by sweet drawings and doodles in coloured ink. The early poems are written in large, round childish script. As she gets older, the script becomes smaller and more flowing. When I read these poems—now kept in the National Library of Australia—I was reminded of *The Children's Treasury of Verse* or similar anthologies which I knew as a child and which many generations of English-speaking children have known. They are full of poems by Robert Louis Stevenson (which he wrote specifically for children) and works by well-known poets considered appropriate for children, such as William Wordsworth's 'Daffodils', William Blake's 'Songs of Innocence', Edgar Allan Poe's 'Eldorado', Lord Alfred Tennyson's 'The Eagle' or 'Break, Break, Break', Christina Rossetti's 'Hurt No Living Thing'. Poems Judith's parents had read to her and her brothers. Not surprisingly, her first poems are derivative of this kind of verse.

There are a number of poems amongst the later juvenilia that show a growing preoccupation with death. It may simply have been that she was at an age when we first begin to grapple with our mortality, or that she was reading a lot of late Victorian poetry, with its melancholy, and sometimes sentimental, obsession with death. (Her mother kept a scrapbook of her favourite poems which particularly influenced Judith's early writing. She would later tell Meredith that she wrote as much to please her mother as for herself.) While none of her juvenile poems can be definitively said to be about her mother's death, there is no doubt that many of them are grounded in personal experience. At this time, she was consciously learning her craft by experimenting with existing forms, forms that could both transform ordinary experience and channel intense emotion. These poems show an acute awareness of death's finality and pointed references to the pain of being separated from one's mother, even if this mother is figured as 'mother nature'. A poem such as 'The Battle' imagines a battlefield from nature's point of view: 'Have they dared to trample your breast mother, my mother?' The poem is narrated by the night that falls like a healing balm, offering comfort.

Dead trees lament the fact that they will never feel the 'green sap run / in their arms again' or 'feel the keen breeze blowing ever' in her poem 'Never'. The refrain, 'Never—never—never again' hauntingly prefigures one of Judith's most moving, mature poems, in which she finally came out and said what she could not articulate as a young girl. Almost fifty years after her mother's death, when Judith was the 'grey-haired daughter' her mother had never known, she studied her mother's wedding photograph and confessed:

> I know her
> better from this averted girlish face
> than in those memories death cut so short.
>
> That was the most important thing she showed us—
> that pain increases, death is final,
> that people vanish.

In her early to middle phase, when she was in the first flush of love and more intent on celebrating life than thinking deeply about death, Judith often invoked death as an abstract state of non-being, the necessary darkness out of which life springs, part of an on-going cycle. Later, the idea of death served as an occasion to reflect, in a very Buddhist fashion, on how fiercely we cling to notions of 'self' or the 'I' and thus live in terror of our own end. But as her husband, Jack, grew more fragile in the years before his death, Judith once again became preoccupied with death as a pressing reality.

After his death, at her most despairing, she felt that 'since through you I lived / I begin to die'. If she believed in any form of immortality, it was in the afterlife of his work. In her elegy, 'The Vision', she celebrated Jack's life's work as a philosopher and presented his death as a kind of apotheosis in which he achieved the absolute truth he had always sought. Two decades later, as her generation was dying and she was facing up to her own death, her thoughts about it were less exalted, more earthy. Life and death were defined by the flow and transformation of energy. Each individual life was a kind of pathway along which energy flowed. Each followed 'unguessable routes' but all ended at the same point: 'like the wood on the fire, / the wine in the belly.' This, in the end, was what her observations of the natural world had taught her.

New England

ONE

Train Journey

A few hours out of Newcastle, I began looking for signs: outcrops of rocky granite, the bones of an ancient land poking through the surface, the earth splitting open in mighty gorges. 'Clean, lean, hungry country.' There must be a moment, I thought, when you sense that you have entered the New England Tablelands, when the elevation is such that there's no mistaking it: you're in the highest part of the whole country after the Southern Alps. I had inhabited this terrain in my head for thirty years, surely I would know when we had arrived there. 'High delicate outline / of bony slopes wincing under the winter.'

The Hunter River valley undulated lazily until, as we approached Muswellbrook, the land began to shrug its shoulders more often. Only after Scone did these individual hills begin to coalesce into a rolling upland. Small rocky outcrops appeared as the hills grew sharper with substantial eucalypts on the upper slopes, the lower cleared for pasture. The climb, however, was gradual and it was hard to believe that we had reached any great height. I kept willing the landscape to be more dramatic, more like a mountain range. Explorer John Oxley, who had viewed the tableland from the coast, had a similar problem when he ascended the plateau from the west in 1818: how to reconcile his vision of a Great Escarpment—as seen from the coast—with the reality of gentle inland slopes and the upside-down world of the plateaux he discovered.

Slowly, the hills started to gather, hill after hill crowding in to create the impression of a spine, if not a range. Even so, I still felt removed, like a spectator watching it all roll by on a film. This was not my landscape but, having absorbed it through Judith's many poems about New England, I felt that I knew it. And now I was waiting for that flash of recognition when the imagined and the real would come together. 'There it is!' I would say. 'The harsh scarp of the tableland, just as I had imagined it.'

In the seat opposite, my old school friend Cheryl was reading from Judith's *Collected Poems*. Almost thirty years before, Cheryl and I had sat in a large auditorium in East Melbourne listening to Judith give the formal address at our final year speech night. I asked Cheryl whether she remembered much about that night and, in particular, what Judith had talked about.

She laughed sheepishly, 'Not really.'

'Neither do I.'

All I knew (prompted by an article I'd written for the school magazine) was that she'd talked about the dispute at Noonkanbah with the Year 12 Literature class a few weeks before. Cheryl and I agreed that the topic would have probably been this issue, or the environment, or both. It was understandable that Cheryl struggled to remember. For her, Judith had been just another public figure doing what guest speakers do. But I had no excuse for drawing a blank. I was the one who was supposed to be mad on her poetry. What's more, I'd had dinner with her only hours before she addressed the school, and ought to have been more alert. Dinner had been a small affair in the principal's house next door to the school. As I took my seat, I glanced nervously across at Judith, afraid to open my mouth yet longing to say something that might impress her. If she felt the strain of making conversation, she did not show it. While the occasion seemed to demand high seriousness, her impulse was to use dry humour to lighten the mood and avoid topics that were too complex or controversial to be reduced to dinner-party chat. To one of my earnest questions she gave a knowing half-laugh, half-sigh. 'Ah, yes, well, that's a big one, isn't it?'

Later that evening, as she addressed the whole school, I struggled to reconcile the detached, unemotional demeanour of the white-haired woman up there on the podium with the passionate, lyrical intensity of her poetry. Progressive hearing loss had affected the tone of her voice and I worried that people would find her speech a bit dry, her voice lacking in inflection, her manner gruff. What she was saying made the audience uncomfortable, that much I do remember. She wouldn't let anyone off the hook. I sat there willing them to warm to her, to understand that to be a great poet you did not have to be a great performer; that it was the words that mattered not their delivery. Maybe this is why I took in little of what she actually said. I was too busy fretting over the discrepancy between the poet and her poems. Too busy wanting people to appreciate the importance of her presence.

I wasn't aware, then, how the principal, John Shilliday, had stuck his neck out by asking Judith to give the address that night. His instincts were, as it turned out, more progressive than those of many parents who later made it clear they did not approve of his choice. Judith had warned him, when he asked her to come, that she wanted to talk about the work of the Aboriginal Treaty Committee. She suspected, however, that it might be too controversial for an occasion where parents, in her experience, tended to prefer something 'bland and unchallenging'. But, if he were willing to take the risk that her speech may be regarded as 'fire-raising' and 'indoctrination of the young' she would do it. Afterwards, she mentioned the occasion in a letter to Meredith. In typical fashion, she described herself as the 'human sacrifice'. She thought it went well enough: 'A huge important audience of parents as well as girls, song, dance, prayer and all the fixings, and at least I put the story over, so maybe it is not all wasted.'

Sitting on the train as it climbed the imperceptible slope of the New England plateau, I could still see Judith on the stage, could still hear her gravelly voice. The words were gone but they were not wasted. Soon after, the train slipped into a long, dark tunnel and, when we came out the other side, it seemed that we were no longer looking at the hills from a distance but were finally amongst them. Even the sky felt closer. Gigantic cumulus hovered over hills dotted with outcrops of granite. To my surprise, the higher we climbed, the more heavily grazed and cleared the land seemed to become. And the more frequent the white skeletons of trees. Whole paddocks like graveyards. I knew from her juvenile poetry that Judith had been haunted by dead trees since childhood. In her memoir, she reflected on the sight I was now witnessing. Perhaps, she wrote, these dead trees had lost the will to live after what the pastoralists had done to the land. 'They may have given up trying to return and are dying, or dying back, as we call it.'

Since the 1950s, millions of eucalypts have died in the lower parts of central and southern New England because of pasture improvement methods which have led to increased numbers of defoliating insects. When Judith wrote 'Train Journey'—a homecoming poem in which she is returning to New England to visit her family—she may have witnessed the beginnings of dieback. The 'small trees on their uncoloured slope' that flash by her train window are not dead but you sense that they are struggling. Like poetry, they are 'articulate and sharp'. She urges the trees to hold on, to extract all they can from the rocky earth, in the same way that poetry brings the 'unliving' to life through language. The urgency of the poem is a measure of the helplessness she felt. She had no control over what was done to the land she loved—only her brothers inherited the family properties. All she could offer were her words. As she wrote in another poem from this early to middle period called 'Eroded Hills': 'When the last leaf and bird go / let my thoughts stand like trees here.'

The train climbed higher, beyond Walcha Road, and I noticed that even the tops of the hills were now cleared for grazing and the hillsides looked more thinly clothed. Yet hard as I searched for the landscape I had conjured out of words on the page, the one I had inhabited all these years while reading her poetry, the difficulty—perhaps the impossibility—of finding it was beginning to dawn on me. Poet and critic Jennifer Strauss has remarked that especially in her earlier poems, Judith often seems to be 'yearning for the moment of infinity when parallel lines will meet without trace of separation.' The parallel lines of nature, human desire and poetry. A train journey, with its separate tracks, is a powerful reminder of that impossibility. To think that I might find myself stepping off the train and into my imagined landscape was perhaps a similar yearning and a similar folly. The imagined terrain, the real place and the psychological landscape of the poems could illuminate each other, but could they ever meet?

TWO

Jeogla

Caroline was waiting for us on the platform at Armidale station. She put up a hand to catch our attention. A small smiling woman, not much taller than Cheryl and I, in a neat cotton shirt, pressed trousers and sensible shoes. I had met Caroline once before when she and her sister Pip were in Melbourne. The resemblance between Pip, who was Judith's oldest niece, and Judith was striking. To be with her was to experience flashes of Judith as she spoke. The same deep-set eyes, strong jaw and prominent teeth; the same droll, no nonsense take on the world. The resemblance between Caroline, Judith's second niece, and Judith was less obvious but would become more apparent as our week together passed. Whereas Pip, like Judith before her, had fled New England (despite her deep love for it) as soon as she could—had gone into voluntary exile to escape the conservatism of the New England pastoral 'aristocracy', the weight of being one of the Wright clan and the family's traditional expectations of women—Caroline was the one who had stayed behind.

26

'Are you all right now?' I asked after we embraced. Only weeks before we arrived, Caroline had been seriously ill in hospital with a partially collapsed lung. When I'd emailed her about postponing our visit, she wouldn't hear of it. She had everything organised. She would show us around all the major Wright family properties: Wallamumbi, where Judith grew up; Wongwibinda, where the matriarch of the family, May, lived; Thalgarrah, where Judith's mother grew up and Judith was born; and Jeogla, where Pip and Caroline grew up, the property that their father Bruce inherited from his and Judith's father, Phillip.

On the way to her house on the outskirts of Armidale, Caroline took us for a quick tour of the town: through the university which Phillip had helped establish and of which he had been the first chancellor, past the memorial park dedicated to Judith, and past the red and clinkerbrick Edwardian buildings of the New England Girls School where Judith, Pip and Caroline had gone as boarders. Pip and Caroline were always being admonished to 'Remember your aunt' by their English teacher, who had also taught Judith. The Wrights were one of the oldest families in the district and, until the late 1990s, one of the wealthiest and most influential. The achievements of the family are a source of great pride for Caroline. Yet, like Pip and Judith, she remains deeply ambivalent about the family's traditional attitudes towards its women.

When we visited Jeogla the next day, I began to appreciate the complexity of Caroline's—and, by implication, Judith's—relationship with these family properties. Judith did not write about this property but she spent a lot of time here while she was in New England during the war, doting on Pip and escaping from her stepmother, Dora, with whom she did not get along.

As we drove up the poplar-fringed road to Jeogla, Caroline pointed to the creek where she and Pip cultivated secret gardens when they were girls. The actual garden around the house—much expanded since Caroline lived here—is European with lime green lawns and garden beds and shady nooks, like a moat separating the inhabitants from the stark, open paddocks and clumps of native bushes and trees.

'It's lovely to see all the eucalypts looking so healthy,' she beamed. A long drought had recently broken, making everything unexpectedly lush. 'It hasn't been like this for ages.'

We stopped to open the gate. When Judith was living in Queensland with Jack, she would occasionally come to visit. Pip and Caroline would be allowed to go and sit on this gatepost to wait.

'It was always exciting when visitors came because we were so isolated. Judith and Jack always owned old cars. They never seemed to pack suitcases. They opened the back of the car and chucked everything in.'

Caroline had not been back to Jeogla in ten years, not since it passed out of Wright hands in 1998 after her younger brother Richard's business went into receivership. The loss of Jeogla from the family marked the beginning of the end of one branch of the Wright pastoral dynasty. Our visit was, therefore, something of a homecoming for her. The people who now own the property were out but had told Caroline that we were free to roam about the garden. Above all, Caroline wanted to find the plaques where her parents' ashes had been buried. She thought she remembered the spot but changes in the garden layout left her uncertain.

As I watched her searching for what remained of the garden of her childhood, I wondered what ghosts she was encountering. She seemed genuinely pleased about how well it had all been looked after and untroubled by the changes. But I knew that the loss of the property—rolling pasture in every direction giving violent way (as I would soon find out) to spectacular gorges and waterfalls—had been a source of deep sadness.

Her father once told Caroline, 'We don't own the land. We are custodians of it. We can't bequeath it to you. You have a husband who should look after you.' Judith's response to this traditional rural approach to inheritance was to reclaim the land through her poetry. Caroline has maintained her connection by staying close to where she grew up, and now she and her husband, John Mitchell, have their own property.

'I love this country. I get passionate about a tree. Something leaps out at me and I stop and get out of the car and drink it in.'

The growth in the garden was so abundant that Caroline had to give up on her search for the plaque. I was worried that she might be disappointed.

'Does it bother you?'

She shook her head. While she was sick in hospital recently, she had done a lot of hard thinking about the past and about what really mattered. Somebody had asked her how it felt to know that her parents' ashes were in a garden that no longer belonged to her family. She told them that it didn't bother her as it didn't change the past.

'Nobody can take away from me my memories of this place and my love for it. Coming back hasn't upset me at all. It helps to know that the family living here is a very delightful young family. Things move along and that's how it should be.'

Pip had told me some months before that one of the reasons she couldn't go back to Jeogla was she couldn't bear to be reminded of 'that beauty'. Our visit to the house and paddocks surrounding it had showed only one side of the property. The beauty that she spoke of only really made sense to me when we went to Wollomumbi Falls, the steep and dramatic precipice which Jeogla backs on to. The falls were once considered the tallest in Australia.

When driving along the main roads, all you can see are gentle hills and paddocks nursing granite boulders like prehistoric eggs. There are times when the granite outcrops look like something the earth is trying to expel, some form of irritation or foreign object or shameful secret that it needs to be rid of. It is deceptive, mysterious terrain. You can think you have its measure only to suddenly find it falling away at your feet.

A short drive from Jeogla, we took a turn-off that ended at a small carpark. There, before us, the land cracked open in a massive granite gorge, a drop of two hundred and thirty metres that had been cut into the flat-topped plateau by millions of years of erosion. A thin white skein of water hung from the top of the precipice and fell in a multitude of continuous, invisible threads to end in a tangle of foam in the brown Wollomombi River below.

'That's Jeogla on the other side.' Caroline pointed to the land behind the waterfall. I stood, gaping. What an incredible thing to have at the bottom of your backyard. I remembered what Pip had said about the times she had spent riding with her father around the top of the property and how thrilling it was to suddenly come upon the gorge.

While we stood there, Caroline told me the story of the woman who lived in a house on Jeogla near the gorge boundary—the 'bottom end', as it was always called. The woman, her husband and his brother spent their days fixing the fences and rarely ventured off the property. One day, the woman didn't return to the house in the evening. Everyone was sure she must have fallen into the gorge or that she would die of exposure overnight. The next day, she wandered out of the bush having slept in a hollow log.

In this way, Caroline peopled the landscape for us with her tales, just as Judith had in her many early poems about the bullocky and the remittance man and the mad old girl who retreats behind her hawthorn hedge and the half-caste girl and Old Dan in 'South of My Days'; poems in which the region's colonial history is brought to life, always exploring the tension between the individual and the land.

South of my days' circle
I know it dark against the stars, the high lean country
full of old stories that still go walking in my sleep.

That evening over dinner, John Mitchell asked about what we had done that day. He has a slow, deliberate way of speaking which disguises a sharp and compassionate legal mind. His bemusement with the Wright family saga was plain. Everyone who is not of the family but connected with it, I would discover, lives in its shadow to some degree and must contend with its myths and baggage.

We talked about Judith's need to get away from New England after she finished school and how she didn't get on with her stepmother, Dora.

'Tomorrow I'll show you a very special rock that Judith used to take Dad [Judith's brother, Bruce] to when they had major problems with Dora,' Caroline promised. 'Judith would say, "We have to have a council meeting." And they would leave the house and go down to Council Rock and have a talk about what was going on and make a bit of a game plan.'

THREE

Council Rock

Rain had been forecast but for now the sun was shining through scattered clouds. We were at a point in the road that offered a clear view over Wallamumbi, the sheep and cattle station where Judith had grown up, fifty kilometres from Armidale. Caroline pulled over so I could take a photograph.

'I still get a catch in my throat when I look at it,' she said. 'Then you have to remind yourself that nothing is forever.'

She was remembering visits as a girl, the joy of seeing her grandfather, Phillip (Judith's father), with his barrel chest and arms spread wide in greeting. And the anxiety of knowing that Dora, her stepgrandmother, would be waiting with a medicinal spoonful of molasses.

Slowly, we drove through the outer paddocks and past a regiment of poplars until we found ourselves gently descending into the 'mysterious valley' Judith had written of, the land of her childhood.

There was a wooden bridge over a creek, and I knew it must be House Creek and that Council Rock would be nearby.

'There it is,' Caroline said, pulling over again.

We all got out. There were willows down by the creek, just as Judith had described, but the banks were richly grassy and green. This greenness everywhere was starting to feel uncanny, like a cloak disguising the true country beneath. Judith's early mature poetry had been written in the wake of a severe drought that had turned the landscape to dust. She wrote of dust eclipsing the sun and the 'steel-shocked earth' turning against the plough. This had happened because mankind had dreamed the 'wrong dream', a dream of domination over the earth. The result was both the destruction of the land and the devastation wrought by the Second World War, with its 'eroding gale that scatters our sons'. If there was to be any hope for the future, she believed, there needed to be a change of attitude, a new way of thinking about our relationship with the land.

Since the turn of the millennium, New England had been again parched by an eight-year drought until it broke, dramatically, only months before our arrival. Everyone kept telling me that the countryside didn't normally look so well fed and watered, and that I ought to come back in winter when the bones would be poking through. Although a little disappointed that the landscape was refusing to neatly replicate what I had imagined, I couldn't help feasting on the greenness. The countryside around Melbourne where I lived was blonde and knuckle-bare and I knew too well how drought could bleach the land until it threatened to blow away. Yet what I was seeing here was an aberration brought on by freak rainfall and modern fertilisers. What Judith had experienced and foreseen back in the early 1940s was, in fact, closer to the reality facing us now. Every time I read an article or book on climate change and its likely impact, I would hear Judith's voice tolling in my head. Green as her valley looked now, it was my hope that being here would help me better understand the bony landscape of her youth, and how it had helped her see so far ahead of her generation.

We stopped in the shade of an old oak tree. Before us loomed a massive granite boulder that brought to mind a humped-back animal heaving out of the earth. There was a pleasing symmetry in its relationship with the surroundings, positioned as it was by the creek, the willows and the nearby bridge like a solitary—if very large—stone in a Japanese garden. I could see how it would appeal to children, how it could become a special place. It was screened by a thick stand of pines and poplars and therefore out of sight of the house further up the hill. When she was ten, Judith captured it's secluded appeal:

> I know a quiet pool where the rushes grow
> And willows overshadow, drooping low
> As if to kiss the water cool and pure.

On this rock by the sandy-bottomed creek, she and her brothers were free to do as they pleased. Perhaps they had once even scratched their initials into the granite. Now, the top surface was covered with large patches of moss and lichen and tufts of grass, like barnacles on a whale. And the way the rock seemed to be lifting out of the ground suggested that much of its bulk was hidden below, making it a perfect metaphor for a poem.

Other boulders of various sizes were scattered nearby. When Judith was a child, blackberry bushes grew wild around all these rocks which were, to her young mind, 'like an assemblage of personalities, whose shapes and surfaces made each of them recognisable.' But it was the largest and most impressive of these rocks that she was drawn to. Her deep affection for this great rock can be felt in the tender detail with which she later described it. She remembered vividly its seat-like shape above a sloping platform, the hollow where water gathered in the middle, and the crack out of which a black snake sometimes slithered. She remembered how the moss, after rain, would give the rock's grey surface a green glow. She remembered how the granite smelled like sulphur and struck matches in the summer. All of these textures and colours and smells were, she wrote, 'still part of me'.

But, by this stage in her life, Judith felt more keenly than ever that her family had been complicit in robbing the Aboriginal people of New England of their land. The landscape of her childhood had been 'stripped of all its numinous stories and turned into mere "scenery" at best, and pasture at worst'. She remembered the many granite rocks of the region 'with a sense of my own exclusion from their meaning. I was born within their influence, but I do not have any right to their story.' And, yet, as I climbed on to the rock and looked around, imagining Judith standing in this very place, holding her younger brothers in her thrall as she spoke, I felt sure that she had not felt excluded from the rock's meaning back then. She had brought her own meaning to it. She had sensed the authority of the rock and, although she would later insist that the rock must have held greater significance for the Aborigines of the valley, everything I had learned about Judith told me this rock held enormous significance in her life.

The name Judith and her brothers gave to the rock—Council Rock—comes from Rudyard Kipling's *The Jungle Book*. Her parents had a full set of Kipling, which she was familiar with from a young age. In *The Jungle Book*, Council Rock is a hill-top covered with stones and boulders where wolf parents bring their new cubs to be recognised by the pack. When the boy Mowgli, who has been separated from his human parents, is adopted by Father and Mother wolf, he is taken to Council Rock. He is reluctantly accepted by the pack, only after intervention by Bagheera, the panther and Baloo, the bear—both of whom instruct him about the laws of the jungle. Although he is human, Mowgli grows up thinking of himself as one of the pack. He not only understands the language spoken by the wolves and other animals in the jungle but is also taught what Baloo describes as 'the Master-Words', which are words that will allow him to communicate with (and gain the protection of) the birds and the Snake-People and 'all that hunt on four feet, except his own pack'.

It is a story in which to be human is to be Other, even though it confers special powers. Mowgli loves the jungle and loves the freedom and community it gives him. The humans in their nearby village are to be pitied, for they do not understand the language and law of the jungle. Far from being a term for lawlessness or survival of the fittest, as it is commonly understood, the law of the jungle in Kipling is a complex body of learning and behaviours that allow most of the animals to get along. The exceptions are the monkeys who are fickle and uncooperative, aspiring as they do to be more like humans.

I had not read any Kipling as a child. By the time I came to *The Jungle Book*, I was steeped in Judith's life and writing and was able to see what I would not have seen before: that it provided a key to her early understanding of the world and her place in it. An understanding that would become much more sophisticated and philosophically complex as she grew up, yet would remain informed by the relationship with the natural world that Mowgli once knew, and by his experience of loss and alienation when he discovers that he does not really belong either in the pack or the village. In time, Judith too would find herself caught between two worlds when, with the death of her mother, she was cut off from the world of childhood and, with her father's re-marriage, she became increasingly estranged from the world of her pastoralist family as well.

But it wasn't simply her affinity with Mowgli, the archetypal 'wild boy', that was significant. When playing on the rock with her brothers, Judith also imagined herself as Mowgli's teacher. In effect, she was in possession of the Master-Words and able to pass them on. These games began when she was five or six, around the time she began writing poetry but before any of it was published in the children's page of the *Sydney Mail*. On the rock, her brothers—whom she regarded as her 'inferiors'—were relegated to the lower platform 'while I lectured and commanded'. Here, Judith found her first audience (apart from her mother) and had her first taste of what language can do. In her recollections, she skips over this experience quite lightly as an example of the bossy older sister taking advantage of her position in the pecking order. But clearly much more was going on.

Her brother, Peter Wright, later recalled that during these games on Council Rock, Judith would strike the granite with a piece of iron and raise sparks, claiming that she had magical powers. It is an electrifying glimpse of the very young Judith in the process of discovering the extraordinary power of language and her ability to wield it; a moment or series of moments during which she felt that anything was possible. According to Caroline, the children were still coming down to the rock when Judith was twelve or thirteen, after their mother's death and father's re-marriage. At least here, Judith had a control over events that she lacked up in the house, her stepmother's domain. Here, she had tasted the potency of the word and, here, her word still carried weight. When she was thirteen, she wrote a poem from the perspective of Thor, the thunder god, which is full of the bravado and confidence that would have characterised her rule at Council Rock:

> Who dares challenge me?
> Ye, the little, petty ones,
> I am lord of earth and sea,
> I am king of storms and suns,
> I am Thor, thunder-god,
> And from my voice the bravest runs.

She didn't always imagine herself as the voice of authority, though, and would adopt the perspective of all kinds of plants, animals and ordinary people. The great beauty of writing poetry, she had discovered, was that it allowed her complete freedom to go wherever she chose, to enter the consciousness of any living or imagined being, to become the voice of nature, to wield the Master-Words.

The stage was set for disillusion.

Thirty years after those early games on Council Rock, Judith declared what she saw as a crisis in language; a conviction deeply influenced by the views of her husband, Jack McKinney. Jack, over twenty years Judith's senior, was a maverick thinker who challenged the dominant trends in post-war philosophy. Drawing on Jack's analysis of how language enabled humans to develop a shared understanding of the world, Judith argued that the word had lost the emotional and symbolic force it once had in primitive times. In the beginning, when humans developed words to describe the visible, concrete world, they did not objectify nature so much as *live* it. The environment was experienced as an extension of human emotions, sensations and intuitions of the divine. At this time 'men and women experienced the sacred in earthly objects, so that symbol and the sacred [were] inseparable,' says writer Karen Armstrong.

But, over the centuries, it seemed to Judith our knowledge and understanding of the world had grown fiercely analytical and abstract, breaking down this intimate connection between the word and the thing. As a result, 'the object has, in a sense, died out of our immediate experience, being replaced by a word-idea.' On top of this, as human thought became more specialised, so did language. Each discipline evolved its own jargon intelligible only to the cognoscenti. More complex and compartmentalised than ever before, human experience had outstripped language's ability to capture it. Modern writers such as James Joyce responded by pushing language to its very limits. But, in doing so, they amplified the work's obscurity. This communication breakdown, this failure of language to meet the demands placed upon it, had happened, Judith argued, because we had lost touch with the living earth which is 'the source of life and language'. Not only were humans alienated from the land but also from any emotional understanding of our place in the cosmos. It was the poet's responsibility, she felt, to revitalise the language and help forge a new kind of consciousness.

When I think of this Herculean task she set herself and all poets, an image comes to mind of her standing like Atlas with a great granite rock balanced on her shoulders. For this was, metaphorically speaking, the emotional baggage she carried with her: the legacy of Council Rock and the promise it had once held for her.

Many of her poems from the 1950s testify to her growing preoccupation with the limitations of language and rational analysis, as she wistfully acknowledges her sense of exclusion from nature's language. In poems such as 'Gum-Trees Stripping', 'Scribbly Gum' and 'For Precision' can be heard her nostalgia for the pre-modern experience of the world, and the echo of that early desire to possess the Master-Words, the Rosetta Stone of the natural world. This yearning is made explicit in the poem 'Birds', in which she expresses the desire to find 'the words that lie behind' all languages, both of man and nature. Torn between two worlds—her family and her new life with Jack—she feels that if only she could leave this battleground for the forest, then she could 'melt the past, the present and the future in one / and find the words that lie behind all these languages.'

In the early 1960s, during a visit to Wallamumbi, Judith sat by House Creek and recalled how she had once walked bare-foot through the cool water and collected ruby and cloud-coloured pebbles. Pebbles which, when dry and left to gather dust on a shelf, lost the lustre they had in the water. As a girl, she had written poetry without inhibition, without this anxiety that her words were 'heavy and dull' like the stones removed from their natural setting. She had once believed 'any poem might follow my pen'. Now she knew that 'the ungathered alone stays beautiful / and the best poem is the poem I never wrote.'

As I sat on the mossy rump of the rock and ate a sandwich, I thought of the biographer Richard Holmes who, when travelling in the footsteps of Robert Louis Stevenson through the Cevennes mountains in southern France, became gripped by the premonition that Stevenson was waiting for him, in person. The sensation was so powerful it was 'almost like a hallucination', he wrote in his book *Footsteps*. But when he reached a bridge he believed Stevenson had crossed, he looked up the river and saw the original old bridge of the village, broken and matted with ivy. This was the one that Stevenson would have crossed. Holmes' conviction that he would somehow encounter Stevenson suddenly evaporated. 'There was no way of following him, no way of meeting him. His bridge was down. It was beyond my reach over time, and this was the true sad sign.'

Over eighty years had passed since Judith and her brothers first started to hold council on the rock. She and her brothers were dead. Wallamumbi was no longer in the Wright family and no one was even living on the property. It was currently looked after by a manager who lived elsewhere. What I felt most strongly here was not a premonition of a possible encounter with Judith's ghost, but a sharpened awareness of her absence, particularly of the girl whose hair, Pip had told me, was so black it shone blue in the sunlight. I had known the white-haired older woman but not the girl.

The rock was now an empty stage where almost nothing remained of what had once taken place there: the intense childhood dramas, the performances and games, the dreams dreamed. I wondered what it was I had expected to find. The faint echo of childish voices? An atmosphere charged with emotion? All I could do was be alert to the mood of the rock at this particular moment, and to what might have happened here given the stories I knew. Only later, after I'd had time to reflect, did it occur to me that being alert to echoes from the past was exactly what Judith had done all her life. For her, the countryside was full of echoes, full of absences that went unremarked by most people. She was instinctively attuned to them, like a medium who channels voices from another world. Just as this rock was overlaid with the moss and lichen of stories—from *The Jungle Book* and the Wright children's own folklore—so too was the wider landscape overlaid, for her, with stories and signs of absence.

As a young girl, Judith wrote about these absences or, more precisely, these invisible presences, in the conventional terms she had inherited from European poetry. Her early juvenile poems are full of fairies, goblins and elves hiding in flowers or floating out of pine cones. This is not purely fanciful or wishful thinking. When she wrote 'There's a spirit in each violet / each poppy and each rose' she was reflecting an instinctive animism, sharpened by loneliness and the need to conjure up company. Later juvenile poems, many of which are preoccupied with death and may, as I have suggested, directly relate to her mother's death, allude to other kinds of ghosts. In 'The Garden Ghost', the narrator tells of a 'little grey ghost' which comes to visit a garden it once knew. The opening verse describes the 'wraiths of roses' watching the garden. But the little grey ghost appears to be a separate, singular spirit which 'comes drifting with a sad half smile adown the pathway dim' and 'out the low white gate again she passes, grey and shy.' The pronoun 'she' comes as a jolt in the final sentence and suggests that this is no generic ghost.

The loss of her mother when Judith was twelve wasn't the only factor in making Judith the kind of poet she became. But it can be safely said that Ethel Wright's death made a mind already attuned to 'spirits' in the landscape, painfully sensitive to the experience of loss. Not surprisingly then, she became increasingly aware of other signs of loss and absence in the landscape. Near the woodshed on Wallamumbi was an old tree—now gone—with diamond shapes carved into its bark by the Aborigines who once lived here. She knew also of a bora ring—a ceremonial earthen circle—on her grandmother's property, Wongwibinda. There was the nearby goldmining ghost town of Hillgrove full of ruins from the past, and the town of Uralla which boasted the grave of the bushranger Thunderbolt, who was famous in this region. Everywhere you looked, if you had the eyes to see them, there were traces of the past in the landscape. And there were the stories that went with them: stories of Aborigines driven off nearby Nigger's Leap by vengeful settlers, stories of convicts and settlers, of bushrangers and no-hopers and ordinary people gone mad in the bush, of bullockies and drovers, of her pastoralist family and her forebears. Her first mature collection, published in 1946, *The Moving Image* is haunted by these hidden presences and, above all, by the silence history had consigned them to.

At some stage, when she struck sparks from Council Rock with her piece of iron and declared that she had magical powers, it must have dawned on Judith that she could give voice to these silences. Not surprisingly, she would come to think of silence as the foundation stone on which her poetry was built. Over two decades later she would write:

> Silence is the rock where I shall stand.
> Oh, when I strike it with my hand
> may the artesian waters spring
> from that dark source I long to find.

Silence was her rock, and not only because it contained all that had gone unsaid or might yet be said. Silence encompasses that which exists outside language. Anyone who deals in words, anyone who has ever tried and failed to say exactly what they feel or intuit, knows that we are all capable of ideas and experiences that exceed our grasp and ability to express. It has been argued that when we come up against the limitations of language, we are confronted with the ineffable, an intuition of a transcendent dimension. Whatever we choose to call it—God or the unconscious—Judith knew that it was from this unfathomable silence that inspiration springs and on which poetry is built.

On a more literal level, it is not surprising that someone who suffered from progressive hearing loss should become acutely sensitive to the silence of others, to silences in the landscape and to the prospect of falling into that silence. In poem after poem she would reflect on the fraught business of translating the silence of nature, of the dead, of the rejected and the forgotten, into words.

As we prepared to leave the rock that morning, storm clouds gathered over the Snowies. Down near the creek I spotted movement by one of the poplars and saw, at the base of its trunk, a giant lizard, probably a bearded dragon. Sensing me, it froze; its streaked pewter and black head held motionless, its legs blending with the gnarled grey trunk. For minutes it remained this way, willing itself into invisibility. After admiring and photographing it, we turned our backs to release the creature from our gaze. When it had disappeared into the undergrowth, we joked about it being a visitation from Judith. It seemed the kind of creature she might return as, with its fierce intensity, its alertness and chameleon-like ability to blend into the landscape.

We were walking back towards the car when Caroline suddenly bent down and plucked something from the grass. She held it up, grinning broadly. It was a four-leafed clover.

'Thank you, Doo,' she said. 'Duda' was what Judith's younger brothers, unable to pronounce her name, had called her as young children. To Caroline, Judith had always been Doo.

Cheryl and I scoured the surrounding grass but couldn't find another.

Distant thunder rumbled like the sound of horses galloping over the hills. We climbed into the car, hoping the rain clouds over the Snowies wouldn't come our way, and headed up the driveway towards the house.

FOUR

The Lost Garden

Up past the thick copse of pines and poplars that screened Council Rock from the house, the valley opened out into rolling pastures dotted with trees and panoramic views of surrounding countryside and the deep blue Snowies on the horizon. There was a sudden air of expansiveness, of arriving at the centre of things. If her 'blood's country' had a heartland, this was surely it.

And yet something wasn't quite right. There was no wind and an eerie stillness hung over the place. The rambling weatherboard homestead that Judith grew up in was long gone, replaced by a large, seventies-style brown brick house that lay unoccupied. It was owned by a family who visited only occasionally, leaving a manager to look after day-to-day affairs. We walked around the outside, peering in the windows. Although there was still some furniture in the house, it had a sad and deserted air. Clearly Wallamumbi was no longer a thriving hub or the centre of any child's universe.

In the late 1980s and early 1990s, Judith's half-brother, David (son of Phillip and Dora) borrowed over thirty million dollars to fund an ambitious scheme to make the Wright family Australia's leading supplier of beef. Then a global recession hit, along with a drought. With David's business losing a million a year, the bank called in its loan. In 2000, not long before Judith's death, David lost his legal battle with the bank and Wallamumbi had to be sold. The unravelling of the Wright family's claim to the land and the downfall of this side of the pastoral dynasty would loom large over every place we visited that week; its full implications only registering when we visited Wongwibinda—the original Wright family property bought by Albert and May Wright, Judith's paternal grandparents, in 1888—which was still in Wright hands.

Strangely enough, Wallamumbi's elegiac mood might well have been scripted by Judith herself. Some of her later poetry had anticipated and even predicted the family's fate and their loss of the land. The last time I saw her, before Wallamumbi was sold, she made an unexpectedly vehement remark. 'If I was born with a tassel I'd be there now. I knew from a very early age that I wasn't important in the family. The boys were taught things and I just tagged along. That's very injurious to the psyche.' (No wonder she asserted herself so forcefully over her brothers at Council Rock. It was the one place where her word carried weight.)

When news emerged that Wallamumbi was being repossessed, Judith wrote to Pip and Caroline, reflecting on the sad business of moving everything out of the house. 'I am glad I am not there, I don't think I could bear it, which shows that if I had been Aboriginal and had to leave that country it would have been the death of me.' To David, she is reported to have said, with characteristic bluntness, 'Now you'll understand how the Aborigines feel.'

Yet it was only in the final decades of her life that she publicly articulated these feelings about her family, most confrontingly in her series of poems 'For A Pastoralist Family' which were written in the late 1970s, around the time that David and Bruce Wright split the family's assets, and David began borrowing heavily to fund ambitious new ventures. Judith addressed her brothers in the poem, advising them to remember that they owed their good fortune— including 'the cautious politeness of bankers'—to the hard work of their grandparents and the dispossession of the original inhabitants. Her inheritance, she dryly noted, was not the land but a love of it, which served 'as a base for poetry'.

No doubt aware of her brother's ambitions, Judith warned them of the hazards of getting caught up in 'the heave of the great corporations / whose bellies are never full.' In their departure from the family tradition of being 'A small stream, narrow but clean', she felt her brothers had become sullied by the world of big business, 'All men grow evil with trade'. It is a harsh judgement, softened only by the recognition that no one can truly keep their hands clean. While Judith did not know that David would over-reach himself and that the once 'cautious politeness of bankers' would be withdrawn, she sensed—perhaps more acutely than they—that their grip on the land was tenuous. This, after all, was what her inheritance had taught her: that she had no claim on the land except her love of it.

The irony, I couldn't help thinking as I wandered the garden at Wallamumbi, was that her exclusion from ownership of the property and the inevitable sense of exile this bred was what had made her a poet. As is often the case with those whose great achievement is to transform their personal suffering or pain into a work of art, her loss was our gain. And it was here, in this now-uninhabited garden, that her experience of love and loss began.

Once upon a time, such a loss was unimaginable. 'In our childish years,' she wrote towards the end of her life, 'it would have seemed impossible to believe that even the eldest sons of the family would find a source of dissension and sorrow in the land we loved.' In the final poem of 'For A Pastoralist Family', she makes a plea for forgiveness and lovingly recalls this period of childhood, before questions of inheritance and attitudes to the land came between them:

> Blue early mist in the valley. Apricots
> bowing the orchard trees, flushed red with summer,
> loading bronze-plaqued branches;
> our teeth in those sweet buttock-curves.

While there were few signs left of the orchard that had once stood at the foot of the slope below the house, the yards remained, as did the 'blue ranges' in the distance. We were heading across the lawn, towards a wisteria-covered pergola, when Caroline stopped to get her bearings. Standing with her hands on her hips, she said, 'You've got to remember how much things have changed here. Not just the house but the garden too.'

We looked around. The clay tennis court, where tennis parties were once held on Saturdays—before Judith's mother became too ill to host them—was disappearing beneath weeds. Caroline pointed to an old tankstand near the pergola, partially covered with the abundant foliage of an old grape vine. 'That was there in Judith's day,' she said. It had once created a 'hidden corner' beside the old kitchen wall where Judith could read in peace and not be accused of loafing or ruining her eyes. But most of the original garden was gone, having been dug over and landscaped when the new house was built in the 1970s.

I shouldn't have been surprised, although it was hard not to be disappointed. While I had no expectations of meeting Judith's ghost, clearly part of me had still clung to the idea of the original garden as a kind of enchanted rabbit hole into the land of her childhood. And yet the more I thought about it, the more I realised that the original garden's erasure was sadly fitting. The lost garden of Wallamumbi was emblematic of all that Judith would lose as she grew up.

While her recollections of her grandmother's garden at Wong-wibinda are vivid and detailed, the garden at Wallamumbi endures in her writing in a more impressionistic way, almost as if it were too close for her to see it clearly or with detachment. Its broad sweep is captured in childhood poems such as 'Our Roof', which rings with the confidence and rootedness that comes of knowing one's own special territory, of being queen of all one surveys. Looking down from the roof of the house, the young poet sees the hills, the trees 'stretching away, away'; the clouds in the sky, the sleepy cows and 'the big green garden' with its climbing rose and marigolds and orchard. But although her juvenile poetry delights in her immediate garden, the many different types of flowers and the imagined sprites that live there, its dimensions and layout remain vague. Even the adult poetry tends to go for broad brush-strokes rather than a description of a recognisable place:

> I was born into a coloured country;
> spider-webs in dew on feathered grass,
> mountains blue as wrens,
> valleys cupping sky in like a cradle.

There is a sense that this particular garden is too powerfully connected with her earliest experiences, before the acquisition of language, to ever be reconstructed through words. 'Here where I walk was the green world of a child,' Judith writes in 'The Moving Image'. It is not the physical details of this terrain, this 'lost world', that interest her, so much as the emotions that went with it. She might not be able to make 'felled trees rise upright where they lay', but she can make us experience Wallamumbi as she first knew it. These poems chart a psychological and mythological landscape as much as an actual one. This garden, as seen through the eyes of a very young child, is a magical place where everything is an extension of her own dreams and desires. In poems like 'The World and the Child', the garden is both vast and intimate, a Wonderland viewed by the shrunken Alice. For the child, wild harebell flowers are so abundant they form a blue cave, and an ant climbing a grass blade looks like a monster. The mountain range 'lies like a pillow' for her head at night and the moon swings from the ceiling.

Here, the child is the centre of the universe. As in a naive painting, there is no perspective. The distant mountains—the Snowies on the horizon—feel so close to the child that she rests her head on them when she sleeps. The moon is not some far away celestial body but hangs right above her, like a toy for her delight. This way of seeing the world corresponds with what psychologists call 'the magical years'—roughly the first five years of life—when, according to child psychoanalyst, Selma Fraiberg, the child's conception of the world is a magical one because 'he believes that his actions and his thoughts can bring about events. Later he extends his magic system and finds human attributes in natural phenomena and sees human or supra-human causes for natural events or for ordinary occurrences in his life.' Only gradually does the child acquire knowledge of an objective world until he 'is able to free his observations and his conclusions from the distortions of primitive thought.'

But this rational knowledge inevitably comes at a price, just as it does for Adam and Eve. Part of the adolescent's rebellion is fuelled, as Judith knew too well, by outrage at being expelled from the garden of childhood: 'Only through this pain, this black desire, this anger, / shall you at last return to your lost garden.' It is as if the adult Judith is speaking here to her younger self on whom it has just dawned that hers is to be a double exile: both from the garden of childhood and from Wallamumbi itself.

Just occasionally, as we explored the garden and outhouses that day, the ghostly, flickering presence of the lost Wallamumbi would flare into life. A particularly potent remnant was the original blacksmith's shop where the horses had been shod. It stood, just as Judith had described it in her memoir, under the big pine trees not far from the house. We poked our heads through broken slats in the grey paling walls to find, much to our surprise, the old bellows still there in a dark corner, coated in dust. As a girl, Judith often visited here and was deeply impressed by the 'suck and sigh of the bellows, the glowing and fading of the charcoal' and the black soot that coated everything.

My immediate thought, as I peered through the semi-darkness, was of her much-loved and anthologised poem 'Legend' in which a blacksmith's boy heads off towards the mountains to hunt for a rainbow. He overcomes many obstacles and warnings until night begins to fall, 'ready to swallow him, / like the barrel of a gun'. His rifle breaks and his hat blows away and his dog disappears. But then he sees the rainbow in front of him 'just as his heart foretold'. He catches the colours and the cold of it 'like a bar of ice, like the column of a fountain' and heads home with it swinging on his shoulder, instead of his gun. I had always thought of this poem, which I'd read to my son when he was a toddler, as a fable set in a fairytale landscape, in a faraway time. It had never occurred to me that the story had roots in Judith's own garden and in her daily life as a girl; that beneath the fanciful surface might lie the bones of the landscape she loved.

'I can remember myself a time,' Judith once wrote to a friend, 'when the world was completely animistic to me—every object had a kind of emotional connotation; trees had personalities and water was alive and even furniture lived a life of its own.' This was, of course, the time of magical thinking, the time before the garden was lost. A time which is revisited in this poem where animals speak to the boy, inanimate objects like mountains jump in his way, cobwebs deliberately snatch at his feet, thorn-branches try to make him blind. As he makes his way home with the rainbow, lizards run out to see and snakes make way for him. All the world tells him he is brave. Here is Wallamumbi as the very young Judith would have seen and experienced it—a landscape of adventure and fantasy in which a child could be a hero. Now, as I looked across at the ever-darkening Snowies, I could imagine her as a girl, contemplating the rainbows that would have hung over this range and dreaming of going in pursuit of them.

There was one particular feature of Judith's childhood garden that I knew I would never find no matter how hard I looked. It was the tiny garden at Wallamumbi which Judith herself had created. A garden that persisted in her imagination long after it had disappeared, and that became inseparable, in her mind, from her mother's illness and eventual death.

For earlier generations, the swathe of green around the homestead had played an important psychological, as well as physical, role as a buffer between the homestead and what was perceived as an alien and potentially hostile landscape. Judith remarked once that, for New Englanders, planting a garden meant needing to 'root out everything there already and replace it with roses, delphiniums and petunias and fence it with barbed wire and hedges of conifers.' Yet for all her mature ambivalence about European gardens and New Englanders' inability to see the 'strange beauty' of the indigenous landscape, she remained not only deeply attached to the gardens of her childhood but also to gardening as a way of nurturing the land. Gardens of all kinds and gardening as an activity and a metaphor became enduring preoccupations.

She created her first garden when she was almost four years old. It was a small patch of wildflowers just beyond the garden fence at a drain outlet. In her memoir, she recalls planting the little garden just before she, Bruce and her mother fell ill during the devastating outbreak of influenza in 1919. Although complications from this illness would eventually kill Ethel Wright, Bruce and

Judith recovered unscathed. As Judith felt better, she began fretting about her wildflower garden. When she was finally able to get up, she ran out to check on it and found that it had been demolished by the cows. In another piece of autobiographical writing, she remembers the incident slightly differently. Upon running down to see if the garden had survived, she found a violet there. Her short story, 'The Colour of Death', she says, draws on 'that time of my mother's illness.'

The story comes from the only collection of short stories Judith ever published, *The Nature of Love*, which was first released in 1966. It is about a young girl called Isa who makes a 'secret garden' during a severe drought. She finds a small leak in the house pipeline through the calf paddock, a spot protected from the cows by a growth of sassafras. Her garden consists of wild violets because she is convinced that, without the violets, the spring won't come. Like the young Judith, Isa believes in the magical power of words, and chants a phrase borrowed from their gardener to help the violets grow: 'There ye are now, snug as a bug in a rug.'

Isa's relationship with her invalid mother is a strained one. When her mother is admitted to hospital, Isa goes to stay with her gran. Five weeks later, her mother dies and Isa returns home with her father, whose voice was 'thin and bare, like the grassless ridges where the soil had washed from the clay and pebbles of the subsoil. Like the small half-dead trees that still stood there with roots exposed, he had no shelter to give her.' As soon as she gets home, Isa rushes down to her secret garden. There are two large flowers, 'large as garden violets', and two seed heads swelling on the other stems. In a fit of rage at the world, Isa pulls the buds off and picks the two wild violets. Then she clears the sassafras away so that the cows will be able to see the plant and eat it.

While the story is not simply autobiographical, Isa's mother is clearly based on Ethel Wright, and Isa on Judith. Looking back on this little garden as an adult writing the story, Judith evidently saw a connection between her own urge to nurture the land, and her mother's illness and eventual death. In the story, Isa nurtures her garden in the hope that, with the spring, her sickly mother will recover. Like Isa's mother, Ethel died at the beginning of spring. And similarly, before her death, Judith became increasingly preoccupied with mother nature as something vulnerable that needed protecting:

> Have they dared to trample your breast mother, my
>   mother?
> Have they dared to scorn blossoms bound in your hair?
> Oh Earth, my mother, my mother whose voice cries to
>   the night
> Have comfort, I am the night of healing,
> I kiss your mouth that is fair.
> I hold your hands that are white.

Judith's biographer, Veronica Brady, has observed that 'the land seems in some sense to have replaced her invalid mother fading away in the cold dark house.' The short story shows how this happened by tracing Isa's 'fall' from the garden of childhood into the land of adulthood and the knowledge of death.

There is never one moment when we are expelled from the garden of childhood. It is a gradual exile. Alongside the child's dawning adult consciousness, magical thinking can still persist. For the sake of dramatic unity, however, time is compressed in 'The Colour of Death'. Isa's chant of 'snug as a bug in a rug' over the wild violets she plants is an example of the persistence of magical thinking. Tellingly, it is the kind of thing a mother says to her child when tucking her up in bed. That Judith was keenly aware of the power of a mother's bedside presence to dispel fears is reflected in a poem she wrote when she was ten:

> Isn't it fun when mummy comes
> In the flickery candle-light?
> All the bogies fly when they hear her tread.
> She stoops and kisses the top of my head
> And tucks me up in the nice warm bed
> In the flickery candle-light.

At the end of the story, Isa destroys the garden because her magical thinking fails her. It allowed her to believe that her mother would live if the violets survived until spring. Yet spring came and her mother died. The cycle of life goes on unrelentingly, despite our deepest wishes. After ripping the buds off her wild violets, Isa observes: 'Large as they were, they did not look like garden flowers, real flowers; they had in them a secrecy, a wildness—a knowledge of things that did not happen in gardens, things as fenceless and unknown as death.'

Late in her life, Judith lamented the 'beauties' that had been excluded from the garden of her youth because of the prevailing 'contempt' for native plants. She singled out the native violets as an example of the plants that 'grew outside the garden fences' and were not seen fit for cultivation. This tension between the European flora of the cultivated garden—the idealised garden of childhood— and the wider, wilder native landscape of adulthood is one that all Australians live with. Isa's attempt to cultivate a garden with native violets represents what Judith spent her life trying to do through language and later, more literally, through environmental activism and in her own garden at Mount Tamborine and Edge. And it was in her little garden within the garden at Wallamumbi that this impulse first took root.

Beyond the luminous green of the garden stretched the khaki and yellow of the paddocks. Rain was now falling over the Snowies. We could see it as a filmy ragged mist smudging the horizon, making the mountains appear even darker and bluer than before. It was time to leave Wallamumbi and move on.

The early development of Judith's relationship with this wider, wilder landscape can be traced in the poetry she wrote as a girl and in the few letters that remain from this period of her life. Most of her childhood poems confine themselves to her immediate garden, which almost perfectly replicates the typical garden found in the English literature she would have been reading. Not surprisingly, her poems are full of roses, forget-me-nots, poppies, marigolds, dahlias, larkspur, pear and apple trees, poplars, pines and willows. But it is also apparent that, from quite an early age, Judith was beginning to register the difference between the world of the garden and the world beyond. As well as occasional references to native plants such as wattles, gums and banksias, a few poems venture beyond the garden gate and out into the bush. These poems, which tend to be about the impact of drought and bushfires, are the first signs of the kind of poetry that would make her name as an adult; poetry which invests the landscape with meanings it lacked in the eyes of previous generations.

Unlike the cultivated gardens she writes of, which have the quality of a timeless world untouched by the harsh conditions of life on the New England plateau, the indigenous landscape is seen as much more vulnerable. She knew that bushfires meant blackened gum trees and frightened creatures robbed of their homes. She describes how, after a fire dies down, it leaves a burning track through the 'wounded' bush. Another poem about bushfire and drought describes blue smoke rising from stunted, black trees in the gorges, 'parched brown mosses' panting on boulders, crackling dry grass and an empty creek. One of her few juvenile stories tells of a young wattle tree which admires the fire-blackened coat of an old wattle. The young wattle longs for a similar black coat, but after fire rages through the gorge and there is 'nothing but black smouldering grasses and dying trees', he regrets his wish. In all three cases, fire brings with it the knowledge of death and destruction, just as eating the apple gave Adam and Eve the knowledge of good and evil. This is the knowledge, as Isa puts it in 'The Colour of Death', of 'things that did not happen in gardens'.

After investigating the large shearing shed pungent with the smell of lanolin, we began the drive up Fairburn hill, heading for Wongwibinda. During Judith's childhood, Wongwibinda had been the home of her grandmother, the matriarch of the family, May Wright. Twice a week she rode her horse along this track when she was being schooled by her Aunt Weeta, May's spinster daughter.

Six months before her death, Judith wrote to one of her nieces, asking if she would gather a 'pebble' from the hill of Fairburn Road because 'the top of that hill haunts my dreams'. As we were passing that way, we decided to stop to collect some rocks ourselves. It was gravelly, scrubby terrain with many dead trees on the upper slopes. The sun came out briefly and scalded the backs of our necks as we searched. While I toyed with small, quartz-like stones that looked conventionally attractive, Caroline knew exactly what Judith had in mind.

'Here you are,' she said, handing me two speckled granite rocks, each the size of my fist.

Judith had wanted to be able to smell and hold and examine those granite rocks she so loved. As I write, those two rocks, which make perfect paperweights, sit on my desk and hold open books I am reading. One is made up of coarse, glittering flecks; the other of much finer, more uniform grains with a patch of pale green lichen. They speak to me strongly of that day at Wallamumbi and I can understand why Judith would have treasured them, given how 'alive' inanimate objects could be for her. Each one a miniature Council Rock.

We took the cross-country, four-wheel drive route (now graded but once a narrow track) and, from this elevated vantage point, I began to register the scale of these properties and appreciate the isolation Judith had experienced. Apart from the general store and few houses at the nearby hamlet of Wollomombi, there were few signs of habitation. Pasture with scattered trees stretched in every direction. Away from the bitumen roads with their electrical wires and other signs of civilisation, the landscape ceased to be picturesque scenery viewed from the car window. Here, you could feel its ruggedness, its remoteness, its fragility.

What this native landscape meant to Judith as a girl, and her growing urge to protect it, is strikingly recorded in the few surviving letters from her childhood. All are about an excursion or trip of some kind, to the beach or a favourite picnic spot in the countryside. They were written when she was between ten and twelve—the years immediately before and after her mother's death—and sent (along with poems) to 'Cinderella', the editor of the children's pages of the *Sydney Mail*. Rather than the formality I had expected from an introverted child of the New England pastoral aristocracy, the letters are chatty, full of touching enthusiasm for the natural world and address 'Cinderella' with a child's absolute trust that her observations will be valued.

One can only speculate on the role that 'Cinderella' played in Judith's life as a distant mother figure, but there can be no doubt that she helped foster Judith's dreams of becoming a writer. When 'The Flickering Candle-Light' was published, for instance, it was prefaced with the comment: 'Cinderella considers these verses, which are by no means the first we have had from this little writer, show quite unusual ability. Let us all give Judith a cheer—"Hip, Hip, Hoorah!"'

By the time Judith was nine, she and her mother had lost touch. 'I was shamefully keeping away from the sight of her pain and the changes in her face,' Judith wrote in her memoir. But she still ran to Ethel to show her new poems and letters because her mother had 'ambitions for me as a poet' and took great pleasure when her daughter's work was praised by 'Cinderella'. After Ethel's death, 'Cinderella' was still there, offering praise and encouragement. When Judith won the 'senior' section of the children's page poetry competition, 'Cinderella' declared that 'she is one of the few young writers who have sufficient grasp of metre and those mysterious silent pauses that punctuate it to make use of muted syllables with pleasing effect.'

While Judith thought of herself as an awkward, shy and asocial child, the letters reveal someone else. They bring to mind the half tadpole, half frog frozen in ice that she would describe over fifty years later in her poem 'Halfway'. A creature caught in the process of transformation. One minute the chatty voice of the child, the next the eloquent, precocious voice of the emerging writer. This mix of childishness and maturity makes the letters particularly poignant, especially given the much more guarded quality of her mature correspondence.

What is glaringly absent from the letters, however, is the story of the tragedy that was unfolding at home. Her mother is not mentioned at all and does not appear to have gone on these excursions—presumably she was too sick. In her absence, 'mother nature' fills the breach. Judith tells of a trip to South West Rocks, where the family had a holiday house, and rapturously describes the beauty of the changing landscape along the way: the 'great blotches of purple' false sarsaparilla, the road cut into the mountainside, the sharp bends, a house perched on a cliff top. 'When we looked down there were only chalky white rocks, a few scattered trees, and the wide blue river sailing on sedately and calmly. Here it widened out, and there it narrowed; but it hardly ever changed its pace.' When they got a puncture, her father 'fixed it up in some wonderful way.'

There is such command in her prose that you forget—until you reach the remarks about her father fixing the puncture—that this is the work of a ten year old. Her carefully crafted descriptions indicate she is beginning to comprehend the power that mastery of language gives her—as every writer does at some point—and how it allows her to dwell on life's idyllic moments, recreate scenes of beauty and contentment, and edit out the painful bits.

Two and a half years later, she wrote again to 'Cinderella'. Her mother was now dead. The letter appears to be about another 'happy' excursion, this time to Georges Creek, a much-loved picnic spot at the bottom of a mountain called The Big Hill. She, and presumably her brothers and father, swam in the river and went to sit on a hill to watch the 'mountains go slowly behind us and felt uncommonly pleased with ourselves and the world.' What makes her so pleased, it becomes evident, is not simply the view and the afterglow of the day's activities, but the fact that the 'ferns and flowers and bushes and things down there are protected now.' In the past, Judith had seen people stealing ferns and wildflowers by the car-load, but now that had stopped. Yet the letter ends plaintively, with a question that reverberates with inexpressible grief: 'It is a disgrace the way beautiful things are torn up and then left to die, isn't it?' Here, clearly, is the emerging environmentalist. But here too is the memory of watching her mother fade away, and her feelings of helplessness and guilt. Feelings which were displaced into her writing and later into her work as a conservationist. Her father, Phillip, who campaigned to have the New England National Park established in the early 1930s, set a public example for what the environmentalist can achieve. But underscoring this conscious lesson was the much harder lesson her mother's death taught her. When she gazed out over the countryside of New England, as we were doing now from the hill on the Fairburn Road, she saw not only much-loved countryside but a fragile motherland: 'your delicate dry breasts, country that built my heart.'

Real gardens and landscapes are subject to change, they can die or flourish or be utterly transformed, but our lost gardens remain untouched and we can revisit them whenever we have the need. This was surely Judith's consolation. She might be denied any claim on Wallamumbi itself, but she would always carry her lost garden with her and would continue to stake her claim to it through her poetry. And not simply to the properties she knew and loved but to the whole of New England. As A.D. Hope observed, 'New England is an idea in the heart and mind. Judith Wright may be said to have created it in poetry as her forefathers helped to create it in fact and as her own father Phillip A. Wright did so much to create it politically.' She made this claim most forcefully in her poem 'For New England' by audaciously erasing any distinction between herself and the land:

> All the hills' gathered waters feed my seas
> who am the swimmer and the mountain river;
> and the long slopes' concurrence is my flesh
> who am the gazer and the land I stare on.

On her return to New England from Sydney during the war, as the train 'panted up the foothills' she found herself 'suddenly and sharply aware of it as "my country". These hills and valleys were— not mine, but me . . .'

In the face of a society that holds private property to be sacred, Judith swept aside questions of ownership with a claim more fundamental than any legal right. 'These hill and valleys were—not mine, but me . . .' The poetry that flowed from this insight did more than express her own identification with, and feelings for, the land. It staked out a landscape that could never be taken from her, could never be lost. And, by making this landscape part of the collective consciousness and culture of the nation, her poetry created a place that belongs to all of us.

FIVE

Generations of Women

It came as a surprise to find Wongwibinda a hive of activity after the deserted air of Wallamumbi and the solitude of our cross-country drive through the properties that separated Judith's old home from that of her grandmother. Sally Wright had a long table laid out for lunch in the light-filled, covered-in veranda at the front of the house. Tradesmen who had come to fix the roofing wandered through the garden. Edward Wright, the great grandson of May Wright and cousin of Judith, had just arrived from another part of the property to have lunch with us and show us around.

Looking over the above paragraph, I am tempted to delete 'hive of activity' and find a less clichéd phrase. But 'hive' is too apt. Whenever Judith wrote about Wongwibinda, May was the queen bee around which everything revolved: 'If she had wanted her children and grandchildren to remember their childhood as a sort of accompaniment to their grandmother's garden, with her at its centre, she had certainly succeeded. Even now the scents of lavender, heliotrope and clove pinks seize my memory with the presence of those sunny days.' By the time she wrote this, late in life, Judith's feelings about May had become much more ambivalent and critical than they had once been. But, as a child and in the early decades of her writing career, she not only admired May without reservation but also identified with her.

Her poem 'The Garden' imagines May wandering through the garden we were now standing in, 'Walking slow along her garden ways, / a bee grown old at summer's end'. The poem paints the garden with its flowers of red and purple, huge pines, sunlight through the apple tree and a 'humming may-tree'. Even when May herself is not mentioned in these early poems, her totem may-tree stands in for her, invariably humming with bees and vibrant with life.

It was summer's end but I was not conscious of the bees that day. We had come up the driveway darkened by those massive pines and a few oak, walnut and chestnut trees. The pines, planted by May in the early 1890s, had many spiky dead and dying limbs amongst the living branches. When the house appeared at the top of the rise, I felt the satisfaction that comes of finding something just as you had expected, as though you have dreamed it up yourself. Here was the veranda with its crossed wooden rails. Here were the climbing roses and the colourful garden beds. Here was the heart-shaped lawn out the front that Albert had designed for May as a Valentine's gift. It wasn't until I stood back and examined the house and its surrounds more closely that I registered a subtle change: only half of the heart remained. One side of the driveway—which had circled the lawn and given it its distinctive shape—was gone.

Tempting as it was to see some significance in the 'broken' heart of the 'Wongwibinda' front lawn, there was none. This property was, after all, one of the few that remained in Wright hands precisely because this side of the family had never risked the expansion embarked upon by Judith's half-brother, David, when he had tried to follow in May's ambitious footsteps.

Over lunch, when I asked why half the heart-shaped lawn was gone, the weight of May's legacy made itself felt. Edward explained that his mother wanted more space for lawn and trees and so had one side of the heart removed. 'I would have liked to have kept it,' he said wistfully. It was at this point in the conversation that Sally became exasperated. I could see that she and May would have made formidable antagonists. She turned to me, her grey bob framing her tanned face. 'The Wrights are always worrying about family history. It's fine to remember the past but you can't live in it.'

Sally was heavily involved in the local Landcare movement, helping with tree plantings, the introduction of dung beetles and the removal of noxious weeds along the highways. Both she and Edward were very mindful of the damage that had been done in the past when previous generations cleared and over-grazed the land. 'In those days, if you had trees you didn't have grass,' Edward said. 'That was the way they saw it.'

After lunch, Edward drove us across the property to the hillside high above the homestead where there is a very small, overgrown graveyard. When we climbed out of the car, he strode forward into the chest high grass that almost completely hid the gravestones and flattened it with great swipes of his arm.

'This is the longest I've ever let the grass grow,' he muttered, slightly mortified that his great-grandparents' graves should look neglected. The pressures of keeping the property going left little time to spare.

On the way up the hill, he had talked about the difficulty of digging graves on this spot because of a granite reef three feet down. You had to bust your way through the rock with a crowbar, cursing the dead as you went. It was Caroline's typically irreverent view that this particular location was chosen for the graveyard only because it was no good for grazing. In *The Generations of Men*, Judith speculates that May picked this spot because 'even in death she must overlook what is being done on her beloved property.' There was, indeed, a fine view over gently sloped pastures towards the homestead, which was little more than a flash of red roof amongst the brilliant green of the European trees that surrounded it.

Once the grass and a large thistle with purple flowers had been pushed aside, we could see the headstone of Charlotte May Wright, flanked by her daughter Weeta on her right—at her side in death as she had always been in life. On her left is the grave of her husband Albert, who had died in Queensland, defeated by the overwhelming demands of keeping their distant cattle and sheep stations afloat. May's stature in the family is reflected in the graves themselves. Hers is the most impressive: a tall headstone of white marble with an engraved dove swooping down toward the fading words. Beneath her birth and death dates is a quote from Corinthians. 'And now abideth faith, hope and love, these three; but the greatest of these is love.' Weeta's headstone is a squat block, while Albert's grave has a prone slab (originally a headstone) that was brought here from Rockhampton where he was buried.

The title of Judith's fictionalised account of Charlotte May and Albert might refer to generations of *men*, but it ends with a eulogy to May, who established the Wright's stronghold in the New England region in the late nineteenth century, and who continued to oversee the affairs of her family and its many properties until her death in 1929. As Judith researched the memoir in the late 1940s, the suppression of 'the real story of the great pastoral invasions of inland Australia' began to dawn on her. But very little had been written about the Aborigines' side of the story, and lacking the time and resources to explore the black perspective, she focused on her immediate family's history.

What she did know was that Albert had considerable knowledge of the customs and languages of the Aborigines he dealt with. Her portrait of him is of a thoughtful and complex character, sensitive to his own role in their dispossession. Around the time of his fiftieth birthday, she imagines Albert reflecting on what the countryside will look like in another fifty years' time and how Paddy, one of the blacks who works for him, will not know his own country because of the clearing of the land. 'That would be partly Albert's own work—his and that of his sons, perhaps, and of his neighbours and their sons. They spent their lives destroying one way of life to make way for another.' It was not until the late 1970s that a three-year fellowship enabled Judith to return to this story and fill in what she saw as the historical, political and cultural gaps in her previous narrative. *The Cry for the Dead*, published in 1981, tells of the devastating impact of the great pastoral migrations (in which her grandparents played a part) on the Aboriginal people.

In *The Generations of Men*, May is portrayed as a shrewd, strong-minded business woman, a loving if strict mother, and a charming, independent and indomitable matriarch without whom the family dynasty would not exist. When Albert died in 1890, leaving her in massive debt, she had been under great pressure to sell up the property and buy a cottage in town and concentrate on educating her four children. But she was determined not to give in. Drawing on her knowledge of the way the property was run, her natural business acumen and her capacity for hard work, she not only brought Wongwibinda through the depression of the 1890s but expanded the family's holdings to include Wallamumbi and Jeogla and a number of other properties in the area. By the time of her death, the Wright family were fully entrenched as New England pastoral aristocracy.

Judith's pride in her grandmother's achievements rings through the final paragraph of *The Generations of Men*:

She is entitled to her triumph, then. No one can rob her of her conquests, of the awe that she is held in, of the love that is rendered to her by right. She may expect, perhaps she does expect, that not only her children but her grandchildren and their children too—for who knows how far ahead the ripples of her influence may travel?—will all carry a certain stamp, a mark that singles out even the most distant or rebellious of them for her own.

Judith obviously felt this stamp from an early age, rebellious though she would become. Even before she fully understood May's stature and achievements as a pastoralist, she felt May's profound influence as a beneficent presence, the tree upon which her children and grandchildren flowered and flourished. As a girl, she wrote a poem called 'May Tree':

> Bright tree, white tree, web of spider's making,
> Tree of mist that the wind has kissed, mist that the
>   dawn is waking.
> Your sky blooms are my blooms, frail as the new moon's
>   ray,
> Tiny blooms, like white silk from looms, children of
>   laughing May.

One of her most ecstatic mature poems about childhood describes a young child wandering off from a noisy gathering to hide amongst the leaves of the 'enfolding, the exulting / may-tree' through which she can feel the sap pulsing as if it were her own blood. Everything goes back to May: whether it is the may-tree as a symbol of spring, the origins of life, or May as the matriarch of the Wright family tree.

Just how important May was to Judith is evident when she identifies May, in the poem 'The Garden', as her prototypical Eve.

Not Eve the archetypal temptress, but Eve after the fall, an old woman enriched by her experience and knowledge of life. In this way, Judith constructed her own myth of origin, a myth she would later partly repudiate but which, in her youth and in the early phase of her poetic career, contributed to her profound sense of place, and of belonging. In 'For New England', Judith places May firmly at the centre of her struggle to reconcile her European heritage with her love of her native land.

May also fed Judith's innate interest in the rhythms of language. Whenever Judith and her brothers stayed with May at Wongwibinda when they were very young, she would read to them for half an hour every night. Judith recalled that her grandmother had a good memory for nursery rhymes and poems. Lear and Carroll were her favourites. 'I remember listening to them with fascination because of the rhythms.' One of the most striking aspects of Judith's early poetry is the boldness of her voice, and the confidence with which she claims the land: '[I] am the gazer and the land I stare on.' In *The Generations of Men*, when Judith wrote of the possessive love that burns in May when she contemplates Wongwibinda, she might well have been writing about herself and her own feelings for the land: 'The place for her was alive, it breathed with her own breath; she would not give it up except in the last extremity.' The bold voice of Judith's early poetry, in which she stakes her claim to the land, owes much to the voice of authority she absorbed from May.

As she grew older, however, Judith's view of her grandmother began to change. In what must have been a slow and painful process, she became more conscious of May's flaws and more ambivalent about her family heritage. Early signs of this change of heart are evident in her poem 'Remembering an Aunt', published in 1966, in which she reflects on how Weeta's talents and hopes for the future were stifled by her domineering mother. Weeta's bedroom, she recalls, was 'supervised by her mother's window'. Her hands were blackened from housework, her paintings, which spoke of her aspirations for another life—'Rome / Florence, the galleries she saw at thirty'—were hung face to the wall. Now, it was Weeta whom Judith praised, not May:

> I praise her for her silence and her pride;
> art lay in both. Yet in her, all the same,
> sometimes there sprang a small unnoticed flame—
> grief too unseen, resentment too denied.

What Judith sensed in her aunt is reinforced by a remarkable letter Weeta wrote to Phillip Wright when Judith fell pregnant with Meredith in 1949. Phillip and other members of the family were deeply distressed and shocked by the pregnancy because Judith wasn't married. But Weeta rebuked her brother for calling Judith selfish:

> In reality, she is one of the most fortunate people in the world. Only one person in millions has the great happiness that has been given to her. While we are on earth we are like half-blind children groping about in the dark. The things that we think real and important are only shadows, and we cannot see the real things. Some day when we are in the light and can see clearly, we will know what we look on now as a sorry business is really the most wonderful and beautiful thing that could happen to Duda, and we ought to be most thankful for it.

In Judith's memoir, there is little sign of the awe and respect she had once felt for May. Knowing that Albert's final illness was brought on by exhaustion and despair, Judith speculates about the pressure on him to meet the bank loan to pay for May's dream house at Wongwibinda. 'He may have worried himself literally to death in the face of his determination to give his pretty wife her way.' She also concludes that May's reputation as a good stock manager was the result of 'the vagaries of the market' rather than her skills and knowledge. This revised view is of a piece with her growing disenchantment with her pastoralist ancestors, particularly their treatment of the land and the Aboriginal people. As the focus of Judith's activism switched from environmental to Aboriginal issues in the 1970s, May's paternalistic attitude towards the Aborigines she encountered while living in Queensland would have become repugnant to her grand-daughter. While May's own memoir reveals her to have been a sometimes sympathetic and keen observer of the Aborigines who camped near her homestead, she clearly thought them less than human.

Another reason for the change in Judith's feelings for her grandmother probably had to do with May's contradictions as a role model. Her example showed the young Judith what a woman with brains and determination can achieve, despite the attitudes of the day. And yet May did not grant her daughters or grand-daughters the same opportunities that she herself had. It is one of the great ironies of this family saga that May, who took such pride defying prevailing expectations of her as a woman and in proving herself to be as capable as any man in managing the family properties, did not break with convention and allow her daughters to prove themselves in a similar manner. For all her strength of character, she remained a woman of her time in regard to matters of inheritance. Weeta might have denied her own needs and aspirations by devoting her life to her widowed mother and the household at Wongwibinda, but the Wright properties still went to May's sons.

The last place we visited that day was an outlying paddock of Wongwibinda, known in Judith's day as 'Bora Paddock'. Bora rings are earthen circles on the ground built by Aborigines as ceremonial places where boys of the clans were taken for their initiation into manhood. It was the bora ring in this paddock that inspired her poem of that name, one of her earliest and best-known about Aborigines, or more precisely, about their absence.

Judith had little contact with the remaining Aborigines of New England when she was growing up. She remembers 'only a few dark shadows' visible occasionally on the fringes of their lives: itinerant station hands, stockmen and domestic staff. Her childhood anxiety about a ghostly Aboriginal elder with a spear that hovered in the corners of rooms probably had its origins in an experience of Albert's in Queensland. He was riding in the bush far from their homestead when he came to an open plain with one dead tree in it. A tall black warrior in 'war-paint' standing near the tree beckoned to him. When Albert called out to him in his own language, the man vanished, 'sank into bare plain, as now into time past'. Judith's lack of contact with Aboriginal people and her sensitivity to stories like this would explain why, from her earliest days, she had a sense of Aborigines as ghostly, vanishing figures. As a result, physical traces of Aborigines at the various Wright properties—the bora ring here at Wongwibinda and the tree with Aboriginal carvings near the woolshed at Wallamumbi— would have been all the more haunting for her.

Edward pulled the car over to a spot that looked indistinguishable from any other part of the paddock. We all climbed out and followed him to a featureless patch of grass, just next to a narrow dirt track, within a straggly group of snow and peppermint gums, and the bleached silver trunks of dead trees lying on their side.

'It was around here,' he said.

Many years had passed since he was first shown this site. It would now take more imagination than any of us possessed to detect signs of that earthen ring in this grassy, unremarkable patch of paddock which had since been ploughed.

The song is gone; the dance
is secret with the dancers in the earth,
the ritual useless, and the tribal story
lost in an alien tale.

Only the grass stands up
to mark the dancing-ring: the apple-gums
posture and mime a past corroboree,
murmur a broken chant.

Not even the trees here would have been the ones that Judith wrote about, Edward said. Out of all the places from Judith's childhood we visited, this one was the blankest. The past had been more completely erased here than anywhere else. Which, ironically enough, is what the poem is about—the erasure of Aboriginal life and culture and how it haunts white culture, or at least those sensitive enough to be alert to the signs of what is gone:

Only the rider's heart
halts at a sightless shadow, an unsaid word
that fastens in the blood the ancient curse,
the fear as old as Cain.

At the time of Federation, Aborigines were considered a 'dying race'. But by the mid-twentieth century, it was evident that this was not the case. Today, over five per cent of the New England population is Aboriginal, and aspects of the culture of the region's first inhabitants live on through their descendants. For this reason, the poem is now considered politically naive and even sentimental in its reflection of outdated attitudes that Aborigines are disappearing and that their culture is doomed.

Yet I couldn't help feeling that these criticisms missed the point of the poem. For above all, it is a poem about repression and denial—both psychological and literal. It is about secrets that remain untold, words that remain unsaid. The ground we stood on as we stared uncomprehendingly at this nullified, grassy spot was, in the poem, symbolic of our collective unconscious. And buried in that collective unconscious is the spear of the hunter and the 'painted bodies' which remain with us as 'a dream the world breathed sleeping and forgot'.

Judith wrote 'Bora Ring' in 1944. Since then, much has come out about massacres of Aborigines, and about frontier conflict between whites and blacks. What the poem does most effectively is register the disturbing and pervading silence that existed for so long, especially amongst those who owned the land, about what had gone on. It was at this time that Judith first read Albert's diaries and began to grapple with the dark side of her family history: the degree of the denial required to justify their claim to the land. In *The Generations of Men*, she imagines Albert reflecting on his complicity in the fate of the Aborigines:

To forgive oneself—that was the hardest task. Until the white men could recognise and forgive that deep and festering consciousness of guilt in themselves, they would not forgive the blacks for setting it there. He imagined a whole civilisation haunted, like a house haunted by the ghost of a murdered man buried under it.

SIX

Nigger's Leap

Leaning against the chest-high fence at Point Lookout, we gazed through the branches of snow gums at the misty cloud that billowed up from the valleys below like smoke from a vast cauldron. This was the highest place on the tableland, almost 1600 metres above sea level. When travelling across the rolling hills of the plateau, the elevation of New England was easily forgotten. But here, at this precipitous edge of the eastern escarpment, the world fell sharply, breathtakingly away. This region is known as the Falls Country and much of it is so steep that it can only be entered by horse or on foot.

My stomach plummeted as I peered over the fence. In the deep blue-green canyon below, densely wooded mountains, ravines and pools of foamy cloud spread out before us. Hidden by a thick canopy of trees and vines, the Bellinger, Macleay and Nambucca rivers wound their way seaward to the coast seventy kilometres away where, on clearer days, it was possible to see the waves breaking on the beach and ships passing on the Pacific Ocean.

We stood, quietly mesmerised by the scale of the place and its ancient air of utter indifference to the tiny human figures perched on its rim. Out of the silence rose the ever-boiling vapour from the warm coastal valleys and the occasional tremor of bird song.

'When I was a girl I had a recurring dream,' Caroline said. 'The fence here was much lower then. I would dream I was falling from this cliff and would wake up on the bedroom floor.'

Pip had told me she loved Point Lookout as a girl because it was 'so scary': the sudden drop that 'went down for miles and miles', and then the thrill of taking a walking track and slowly descending into the primal rainforest below with its hanging moss and dripping ferns and waterfalls.

Part of the appeal of places of this kind, it seemed to me as I strained to see further into the valley, is that they are great amphitheatres for our deepest fears and longings, their deceptively carpeted depths exerting a powerful vertiginous pull. Here, we can indulge our dreams of flying and fear of falling and our hunger for wilderness and far horizons without danger. We can give ourselves over to the intoxicating allure of the sublime. It was not hard to see why Judith adored this country. Yet I knew that its significance for her was not simply to do with the awe-inspiring views and operatic grandeur of the landscape. Once you knew what had happened here, your eyes kept being drawn to the 'sheer and limelit granite head' opposite. The series of flat-topped, basalt ridges on the far side of the canyon.

I turned to Caroline. 'Which is it?'

There was no need for her to ask what I meant. She peered through the ever-shifting veils of vapour, straining to see the many spurs that scalloped the northern tip of the escarpment. Finally she pointed to the most naked and sheer of the cliffs that jutted out sharply above the many inaccessible slopes which made up the lowlands.

'That one, I think.'

It was called Darkies' Point. In Judith's day it was also known as Nigger's Leap.

I looked at it and thought of 'the bone and skull / that screamed falling in flesh from the lipped cliff / and then were silent, waiting for the flies.'

We did not have time to descend into the escarpment or for the full day's walk that would have taken us to Wright's Lookout, named after Phillip Wright in recognition of his efforts to have the area declared a National Park. Instead, Caroline took us along the Tea Tree Falls walk, a track some distance back from Point Lookout which runs from the main road into the National Park and provides glimpses of the kind of vegetation that grows in the temperate rainforest below. Every few steps we found ourselves stopping to touch the trunks of Antarctic beeches which were covered in a fleece of brilliant green moss. The long, pale threads of lichen and moss that hung from their branches like great beards brought to mind the Ents, those great sentient trees of Tolkien's *Lord of the Rings*—one of the many glimpses of the magic that Judith and her father had experienced when they came here as children.

When Phillip first camped here with his mother and sisters in the early 1880s, there was no road in. The only way to reach this part of the escarpment was by bullock dray and no one but a few local farmers knew of it. To an eight-year-old boy it must have felt like a wonderful secret. Enthralled by the views, they explored its slopes and the rainforest below. Phillip later remembered this trip as one of the most memorable events of his childhood. He continued the tradition with his own family and, like her father, Judith fell in love with the 'great blue sweep' of the view from the lookout to the sea, the 'mysterious darkness of the rainforest' and the early morning sight of 'a level ocean of cloudtop lapping the very edge of the plateau and luminous with dawn-rose.'

In the late 1920s, at a time when few people gave any thought to conservation or protecting the landscape from development, Phillip Wright began lobbying local politicians and other influential people to have the area around Point Lookout and the Falls Country declared a National Park. When Judith was an adolescent, her father would sometimes bring politicians and other officials camping with the family in order to show them what was at stake. Phillip's discussions with his political allies and opponents introduced Judith 'both to the idea of setting aside such places for their beauty and value, and to the problems of convincing the official mind that such qualities had any importance at all.'

In his submission to the local council, Phillip talked of the huge old red cedars, unique to Australia, but which were rapidly being wiped out. The commercial value of the wood, he argued, was nothing compared with the value of the trees as a 'national asset'. They should be protected as were the giant Sequoias of California. It disturbed him that 'many logs have been cut in the area in years gone by, and are now rotting on the ground.'

These cedars would come to hold special significance for Judith and she would remember them as 'more like gardens in the air, than trees', abundant with orchids and ferns and providing homes for all kinds of birds and insects. In her novel for children, *Range the Mountains High*, a bushranger escorting a woman and her two children through the Falls Country recalls the once-abundant cedars in the ravines and how the cedar-getters had taken most of them. In a direct echo of her father's remarks, the bushranger says: 'Wasted—like that log—you'll see many of them, lying there to rot because the bullock teams couldn't drag them out. In one hundred years' time Australians will curse the cedar-getters; good timber will be as scarce as gold.'

In a sadly ironic twist, the trustees of the New England National Park were later forced to allow logging of the remaining old growth cedars because of lack of government funding after the Second World War. The removal of the old cedars upset the balance between predators and prey that had protected them for so long, and Cedar-tip caterpillars decimated the remaining young cedars. Years later, Judith would remember the 'red wounds in the soil—bleeding in every rainfall' as all that remained of the felled trees.

Our path through the forest finally brought us to the headwaters of the Styx River, where it was little more than a swiftly running creek. We crossed to the other side of the Styx and, as if we had indeed passed into another world, the vegetation abruptly changed—the moist, mossy rainforest giving way to dry sclerophyll species, the snow gum and stringybark that signalled a shift to the high plateau. As we retraced our steps back to the car, I was conscious of how little I had really seen of the park and how superficial my understanding of it was compared with Judith's and Phillip's. I was a tourist here and could never hope to feel the connection with, or responsibility for, this country that they had known and loved so passionately. Nor could I feel the very personal guilt that Judith carried all her life about what early settlers like her ancestors had done here over one hundred and fifty years before.

Judith first learned about what had happened at Darkies' Point when she was back in New England during the war. One day she went with her father, who was in charge of civil defence for the New England region, to search for an old track leading from the tableland to the coast that might be used to evacuate people if necessary. Their search took them to the plateau's edge at Point Lookout. As they stood looking across at Darkies' Point, she asked him how it got its name. He told her that in retribution for the spearing of cattle, early white settlers had driven a group of Aboriginal men, women and children over the cliff.

The shock Judith felt on hearing this story can be gauged through the poem she wrote about the massacre a few years later. From the first line of 'Nigger's Leap, New England' there is a feeling of disorientation and foreboding. It begins with a vertiginous description of the eastward spurs tipping 'backward from the sun' as night falls—a physical sensation which, through the course of the poem becomes a kind of historical vertigo; a feeling that nothing about the past is stable; a feeling of having been set frighteningly adrift. The poem's many jolting shifts of perspective and mood underscore Judith's bewildered sense that her own history has been cast in a new and disturbing light. When she asks, 'Did we not know their blood channelled our rivers?' and then replies, 'We should have known . . .', we can hear her struggling with the guilt that was to become inseparable from her love of the place; her horror that she had been coming here all these years in a state of false innocence, unable to see what was in front of her eyes. This place which she felt a personal claim to because her father had been instrumental in protecting it; this place that laid bare the geological mysteries of the tableland; this place where she had camped since childhood and which had produced 'times of bliss' was now irrevocably changed. The whole atmosphere, the mood, the feeling of it had darkened.

When Judith was researching *The Cry for the Dead* over thirty years on, she could not find any written reference to the Darkies' Point massacre. But she did later acknowledge the discovery of an account by an early settler called F. Eldershaw, whose station on the north-western side of New England was attacked by Aborigines in 1841 and who lead a reprisal raid that tallies with known details of the Darkies' Point massacre.

In the early nineteenth century, as the early settlers began pushing inland from the central New South Wales coast in search of new grazing land and outward from the tableland of New England, the Aboriginal people of the region retreated into the Falls Country. Deprived of their original hunting grounds and the vegetation which made up a large part of their diet, starving Aborigines stole cattle and sheep and sometimes killed the shepherds looking after them. In retaliation, parties of white settlers would hunt them down.

Eldershaw's florid and self-justifying account, with the retrospectively chilling title *Australia As It Really Is*, makes grim reading. On discovering that three shepherds at an outstation had been killed by Djungutti Aborigines and 2000 sheep taken, Eldershaw gathered a party of ten men to pursue 'the murderous villains'. 'Each of our men was savagely anxious and eager to be chosen for this painfully imperative task; the thought of their butchered comrades, with sundry vivid reminiscences of personal escapes from a fate as dreadful, made them pant for an opportunity of vengeance.' By the fourth evening, after a number of skirmishes with the Djungutti, they spotted the Aborigines' camp on a ledge of rock below them. 'Here a scene of most astounding wildness was presented to our gaze; a perfect amphitheatre lay beneath us, formed by a mass of perpendicular rocks, whose bare and rugged faces would have afforded scarcely sufficient room for an eagle's nest.' Eldershaw believed that the Djungutti were attempting to lure them into a trap. From their position above, the whites fired on the Aborigines. The panicked Djungutti began to 'rush in reckless despair towards the only means of escape from their exposed and dangerous elevation.' Screaming and yelling, they were 'urged over the ledge's brink by the pressing crowd behind' from where they fell into 'the yawning sepulchre beneath'.

Eldershaw then claims that the growing darkness prevented him seeing any more of the 'horrid scene'. Yet, he goes on to describe in detail how, when his men moved in, continuing to fire, the remaining blacks 'dashed themselves in frantic violence to the depths beneath'.

Some of the youngest of the tribe hung briefly from the branches of a solitary tree before plummeting to their deaths. 'Sick of the horrid carnage below, I fain would have retired from the dreadful spot, but all my efforts, entreaties, threats, were utterly useless. Shot after shot, with curses wild and deep, the excited fellows launched at their hated foes—their butchered comrades' blood was that night fearfully avenged!'

While disturbed by the carnage he and his men had inflicted, and distancing himself from the worst of it, Eldershaw justifies his actions by turning his version of events into a morality tale in which the natives of the district learn their lesson and renounce all violence. The once 'wild and savage Blackfellow' becomes 'harmless' and 'tractable', winning the 'toleration' and later the 'kind regards' of the local whites. Everyone lives happily ever after.

Much as Eldershaw might have needed to believe this fairytale, his further observations about Aborigines in his book suggest that his conscience was not so easily assuaged. To read page after page of his insistent claims that the Aborigines are doomed to extinction, that they are 'deeply degraded beings', that they have no feeling for others, that they have no religion and are incapable of improvement is to glimpse a man struggling with the intolerable memory of his own barbarity. After mounting his case that Aborigines are subhuman, he describes himself as 'the most sincere well wisher for these unfortunate people'. He then goes on to argue that squatters ought to be entitled to take the law into their own hands—both in self-defence and to exact 'the punishment due to such offences'. The British government owes its subjects 'an indisputable right to protection', he says, regardless of questions about the legitimacy of its claims to possession of 'the wasting territories of such savage tribes'.

While Judith had not read Eldershaw's account, her poem about the massacre reads uncannily like a response to it, for it is as much about the self-justifying mentality behind the massacre and its legacy, as about the massacre itself. Whether she knew that the massacre happened at night is impossible to say, but the poem is pervaded by images of darkness and night. Just as Eldershaw claimed that the darkness stopped him seeing the worst of the carnage, the poem captures the early settlers' willed blindness to what happened, their need for the evidence to remain hidden. Only if we recognise the fact of this repression, confront the darkness of our history and accept (as Eldershaw could not) that 'all men are one man at last', Judith argues, will we be able to move on without being haunted or swamped by the past.

> Night lips the harsh
> scarp of the tableland and cools its granite.
> Night floods us suddenly as history
> that has sunk many islands in its good time.

Tellingly, the same sense of responsibility that fuelled her feelings of personal guilt also provided her with a means of atonement. Years later she would argue that our last chance to make amends was to protect the original beauty of the country. 'It was not "wilderness" to the people who lived by it and through it, but the source of their very life and spirit; and to those of them who somehow survived our invasion it remains so. And for us, too, it can be a place where we find some kind of rest, joy, and even forgiveness.'

There are no graves for the Aborigines killed at Darkies' Point, but Judith surely had in mind their epitaph when she wrote: 'And there they lie that were ourselves writ strange.'

SEVEN

Dreamscape

As she grew older, Judith returned less often to New England, but she never stopped going back to Wallamumbi in her dreams. In part, she was revisiting what she called 'childhood land'—a very specific part of the property which was probably the garden area around Council Rock. But these dreams were not simply a return to the 'lost garden' of childhood. They were always overlaid with adult anxieties about her on-going relationship with this place and her very mixed feelings about her family.

After she began reading Jung in the 1940s, Judith started a dream diary which she kept on and off for decades. Her daughter Meredith still has one of these diaries from the 1960s and 1970s. She showed it to me one evening while I was staying with her at her bush property near Mongarlowe, not far from where Judith lived at Edge. I took the small leather-bound, loose-leaf folder with me to bed and struggled to decipher Judith's handwriting. Many of the dreams recorded were 'big dreams', a phrase used by Jung to describe particularly significant dreams. Big dreams, he said, were not simply personal, they had a universal quality. 'They reveal their significance—quite apart from the subjective impression they make—by their plastic form, which often has a poetic force and beauty. Such dreams occur mostly during the critical phases of life, in early youth, puberty, at the onset of middle age and within sight of death.'

Many of Judith's Wallamumbi dreams happened in the months leading up to Jack's death and involved journeys across the landscape where she would meet people she knew. In one dream, she was at Wallamumbi, walking by moonlight. 'I have walked through fertile country, now I must go into the barren ground among the trees,' she wrote. Her walk took her along a road beyond Wallamumbi which was curiously crowded. Suddenly, she heard her father's voice 'in some long well-reasoned argument' only to discover that he was being broadcast on television. In order to do this, a clergymen had put the aerial-like stake through her father's heart. During her childhood, her father was the voice of authority and reason, and she remained close to him, despite their differences. Yet here, he was a ventriloquist's dummy, his heart sacrificed to make him a mouthpiece for the established order against which Judith was now pitted, and which placed little value on 'unproductive' and quixotic thinkers like Jack. The dream, she reported, left her with a strong feeling of 'going home' with all the 'uneasy reservations that that implies'.

In time, the uneasy reservations of the earlier dream would blossom into full-blown nightmare in which the Eden of her childhood turned feral and ceased to be a place of refuge. She was walking up the drive past the 'office' (where her father worked) near her brothers' room, when a black snake appeared beside the path and lifted its head to strike. Paralysed, Judith allowed it to bite her hand, thinking that once it released her she could run and get a tourniquet. But the snake held on for a long time and tried to bite her again. Despite the implied proximity of her father and brothers, her screams for help went unanswered.

In the months after Jack's death in December 1966, her sense of exclusion from Wallamumbi grew intense. In her mind, it had become hostile country taken over by 'usurpers'. She dreamed that she, along with a busload of other people, were staying in a house on the Fairburn Road at Wallamumbi, effectively kept prisoner by guards associated with the 'rulers'. From the window she could see these authority figures transporting a giant blue cylinder or tower along the road, something related to 'their sinister industry'. When the cylinder exploded, and mist from the explosion began to condense into bright blue chemical powder, Judith became convinced that they were doomed. (She had been reading the environmentalist Paul Ehrlich who had become a household name since the publication of his book *The Population Bomb*, which warned that the world faced mass starvation if its population wasn't curbed. He also warned that everybody would disappear in a cloud of blue steam in twenty years if we didn't mend our ways.)

When a guard tried to persuade her to 'go to a shelter' for the night, she refused to leave. This dream would later find its way into a poem which compares the psyche to a house with handsome front rooms but where 'all the action goes on at the back'—in the unconscious. These rooms are guarded and occupied by 'inner familiars', what Jung would call archetypes. Outside the house are 'the juggernaut machines, / the blue drifting gases, / the crashing aircraft!' The only shelter, in other words, is not an actual place, as beloved as it might once have been, but the dreamhouse of one's own mind.

In 'South of My Days' she had written lovingly of how her 'blood's country' with all its old stories, still went 'walking in my sleep'. Twenty years on, the stories that strode through her sleep were no longer comforting or nostalgic; they were nightmarish visions of environmental disaster, authoritarian rule, danger and dispossession.

Yet Judith clearly had a deep need to be reconciled with her country. Three years after the nightmare in which she was kept prisoner at Wallamumbi, a potent dream signalled the new direction her activism was taking.

She told me a slightly different version of it when I last spoke to her, describing it as an important 'big dream' because it broke down her 'personal fear', a fear that went back to childhood in which a ghostly Aboriginal elder with a spear hovered in the corners of rooms. In the dream, as recorded in her diary, she was at Wallamumbi with her 'father', who was, in fact, an Aboriginal elder. They had come to the end of a journey across countryside with many high rocks. She asked him who owned this country. Her 'father' answered that it had a long history, with successive invasions, but that the 'boxers' had it before they did. (Her friend, the Aboriginal poet Oodgeroo Noonuccal, previously known as Kath Walker, had been married to a boxer.)

As they stared across the flat sandy plain to the ranges in the distance, Judith said to him, 'Look how beautiful the Snowies are in the moonlight with that black band in them.' It is an unforgettable image in a dream of profound significance. A dream that not only held out the possibility of acceptance by the Aboriginal people who had once lived here (despite her family's role in their dispossession), but that also reconciled Judith with her father, who had been—in earlier dreams—an agent of this dispossession. All of which allowed her to finally make peace with her country.

Gazing out at the Snowies, she knew without doubt that it was 'a holy kind of place, there forever'.

Queensland

EIGHT

The Landscape of Love

On this warm spring evening, I could feel the suburb of New Farm exhaling with relief. The working week was over. People were out walking their dogs and having their first drinks on the balconies of restaurants along the waterfront of the Brisbane River. All was green and lush and balmy. The austere landscape of New England felt a world way away.

Every time I visited Brisbane, my friend Anna and I would take this walk to New Farm Park. With its colonial mix of jacaranda trees, jungly banyan figs, flaming poincianas, Edwardian rose gardens and wide green lawns that stretch all the way down to the river, the park is a haven in the middle of suburbia, and much-loved by the locals. As we crossed the jacaranda drive that sweeps around the park, Anna pointed to a gap where some saplings had recently been planted to replace the hundred-year-old trees that had been cut down because they were dying. Their removal, she said, had caused much grief.

Sixty years ago, Judith had admired and written about these trees in her letters. One day, while reading *An Equal Heart and Mind* (the collection of letters between Judith and Jack McKinney from the 1940s), I registered her address—100 Sydney Street, New Farm—and realised I could picture where she was. Or whereabouts. Suddenly, Judith and I had a shared landscape. In her memoir, Judith doesn't say what kind of house she lived in but does mention that the owners were relatively well-off, so I imagined that it might be a large, latticed-work Queenslander, as there are still quite a few of them around New Farm. The room Judith rented was narrow and windowless, but accommodation was hard to come by during the war and she was grateful to have it. I knew there was also a veranda where she sometimes wrote letters while looking out over the park.

Tangled shadows from the jacarandas were stretching across the grass by the time our walk brought us to Sydney Street. Anna had warned me that it was now a barber shop and a cafe. She pointed to a squat, commercial building across the road, with a slab-like orange veranda. Disappointing as it was, I could see why Judith had been pleased with the location and the view. This was no ordinary suburban park. It was the kind of green expanse that a young woman, who had grown up with open countryside in every direction, could take refuge in. There were sports ovals and many flowering trees and artfully constructed rose gardens for which the park was renowned (in Judith's time, there were said to be 20 000 bushes). In the evenings, she would walk around the park before going to bed. Lovely as the roses were, though, they were familiar and European. What made the biggest impression on her were the subtropical flowers, trees and leafy, luxuriant shrubs: their brilliant colours and sweet smells and sheer flamboyance which contrasted so dramatically with the flora she had known in New England.

In her recollections of New England in the early 1940s, Judith recalled the cold and the dust storms during a terrible drought, and her sinking realisation that country life held no future for her, much as she loved the land. Desperate to escape the expectations of the conservative, rural society she had grown up in, she fled to Brisbane in the spring of 1943 and immediately felt as if she had entered a foreign country:

> What I saw now in Queensland was a different kind of beauty—a richer depth of colour, more golden, and warmer air, a darker depth of forests and a deeper blue of mountains and sea . . . As soon as I could travel again, I wanted to look at the new landscapes, the rainforests, the coast with its flowery sand dunes and the plains, to begin again to get in touch with a new way of seeing and writing.

With wartime restrictions on travel, she had to settle for the parcels of nature on offer in the city and occasional visits to the coast.

For all the comfort it offered, this natural fecundity, sensuality and abundance might well have heightened her own feelings of loneliness and sexual frustration had Judith not found a love to match it. Now in her late twenties, she had resigned herself to being 'single and odd'. Her hearing was failing, she was shy and socially awkward. Emotionally she was 'lost in a desolate country'. Yet, within a year of her arrival, she would meet her soul-mate, Jack McKinney, the 'equal heart and mind' with whom she would find the fulfilment and richness she saw all around her in the landscape.

A cloud of lorikeets exploded from a gum tree as we cut across the heart of the park. Near the central rose garden, I saw a young couple stretched out on the grass, the girl resting on her elbow as she looked down at her young man's face. It was a familiar sight in a public park but would have been even more so in wartime, especially given the number of American soldiers stationed in the city. Parks like New Farm and the Botanical Gardens—which was across the road from the Universities Commission where Judith now worked—were a popular refuge for soldiers and their lovers to snatch precious moments together. Judith often saw their 'struggling forms' on her evening walks. Jack and Judith may themselves have 'struggled' in this park, as one of Jack's letters asks Judith if he'd left his tie in her room. 'If not, I left it across the way, in which case—'

Judith's poem 'Botanical Gardens', inspired by this period, leaves no doubt that the explosive blooms and fleshy forms of the plant life in these parks spoke to her of sexual longing and fulfilment. Every flourishing, clambering plant is a metaphor for human bodies in states of embrace: 'the sweet white flesh of lilies, the clutching lips of the vine / the naked flame-trees, their dark limbs curved and strong.' All are 'visions of fulfilled desire' which haunt a life-denying old gardener who once worked in the park. Gardens of this kind would remain places Judith associated with love and sexual longing all her life. When she was away in Sydney for a short period in the late 1970s, she wrote to her lover Nugget Coombs that she had walked through the Botanical Gardens where there were 'two lovely trees in bloom—I wished you could have been there to see them. It would also have added much to my own enjoyment.' We should not be fooled by her formality. Her prose was always much more restrained than her poetry. Flowering trees—particularly the flame tree—held enormous significance for her as symbols of passionate love. Both this comment to Nugget and those to Jack in the 1940s, in which she wished he could see the glorious jacarandas blooming in New Farm Park, were coded ways of expressing sexual longing.

By the time they had become lovers, Jack was living in a nearby suburb, working as a gardener and writing philosophy in his spare time. They lived apart because Jack was still married (although separated), and the social disapproval of broken marriages, sex outside wedlock and the shortage of accommodation made it too difficult for them to live together. Judith would write telling him how much

Judith Wright aged about two
and a half years, 1917.
(The University of New
England & Regional Archives)

Ethel Wright with Judith,
Bruce and Peter, c. 1926
(Courtesy Meredith McKinney)

Judith Wright about 1932.
(The University of New
England & Regional Archives)

Judith Wright and Jack
McKinney with Jack's older
son Graham (left), in New
Farm Park, 1945.
(Courtesy Meredith
McKinney)

'The quiet pool where .../willows overshadow, drooping low' near Council Rock. (Fiona Capp)

The hidden corner by the tank stand at Wallamumbi where Judith would go to read in peace. (Fiona Capp)

Wallamumbi Falls at the 'bottom end' of Jeogla. (Fiona Capp)

The view from Point Lookout across to Nigger's Leap.
(Fiona Capp)

'Calanthe', Judith's house on Mount Tamborine as it is today, shaded by the pre-historic-looking cycads that used to brush the front windows.

Judith with Meredith at Quantum. (Courtesy Meredith McKinney)

Judith and Jack with Meredith and their dog. (Courtesy Meredith McKinney)

Meredith at Quantum in a cot made by Jack. (Courtesy Meredith McKinney)

Cedar Creek Falls, where Judith struggled to remember 'the formula for poetry'. (Fiona Capp)

The author outside Judith's holiday cottage at Boreen Point. (Fiona Capp)

The ghostly paperbarks on the shores of Lake Cootharaba, Boreen Point. (Fiona Capp)

Judith, Meredith McKinney and Nugget Coombs in Darwin in August 1994 during Judith and Nugget's last holiday together in the Northern Territory. (Courtesy Meredith McKinney)

Meredith at the end
of the glass corridor
in Judith's house at
'Edge', 2009.
(Fiona Capp)

Meredith after a swim in the waterhole at 'Edge'.
(Fiona Capp)

she missed him and how she wished he was there with her in the park. This was their shared territory, one of the few places (apart from a secret camp in the bush on the outskirts of Brisbane) where they could be alone together.

Every weekend, Jack would bicycle to New Farm and they would spend long afternoons at the park. A photograph from this time shows them sitting around a rug with Jack's older son, Graham. Jack is stretched out on the grass looking at ease, while Judith is sitting up, half in shadow looking wary, as if uncertain of her position. Behind them is an umbrella-topped poinciana and rows of palms blurred by a strong wind. The books and manuscripts scattered around them are an important reminder that these gardens not only provided them with a space where they could be physically intimate but where they could exchange ideas and dreams of the future. This intellectual exchange was fundamental to their attraction and laid the foundations for everything else. It was many months—possibly even a year—after they were introduced that their 'intense intellectual relationship', says Meredith McKinney, was 'secretly sealed with love'.

Even before they met, they had admired each other's work. Jack, a self-taught philosopher, who had experienced the horrors of the trenches during the First World War, was desperately trying to comprehend the failure of modern thought to prevent another war. While he had little formal training, his suffering gave him the kind of hard won wisdom that cannot be earned at any university. The antithesis of the head-in-the-clouds philosopher, he was someone who had struggled to make a living on the land and who loved to yarn with ordinary people. Judith's close friend Barbara Blackman remembered him as 'a sharp and gentle observer' of the human condition. He was just beginning to outline his theories in a series of essays published in the fledgling magazine *Meanjin*, edited by Clem Christesen, which was then based in Brisbane. In these early editions, Jack came across four of Judith's poems—all of which were responses to the war and the need for a change of heart—and recognised a like-mind.

Judith, for her part, had read Jack's philosophical articles and been impressed. I could easily imagine her excitement, or at least her intense curiosity, when she read Jack's second essay 'The Poet and the Intellectual Environment'. 'The gift of the poet is to *feel* the truth that cannot yet be thought,' he wrote. During such a time of crisis, 'the poetic gift becomes not a mere personal possession, but a profound moral responsibility: on him who possess it fall the ancient mantle of poet and prophet.' Judith's work was already showing that, whether consciously or unconsciously, she felt this responsibility. The exploitation of the earth and consequent dust storms she had witnessed in New England were, she believed, local symptoms of a universal failing that had driven the world to war.

When Jack and Judith were formally introduced at Clem Christesen's home, their intuition that they were on the same wavelength was confirmed. Together they began trying to imagine a new intellectual landscape out of what felt like the ruins of Western thought. It was a grand, quixotic enterprise: two isolated mavericks grappling with what had gone wrong on a philosophical level and what new directions might be taken. Poems from this period show how closely Judith shared Jack's belief in the creative power of the poet to take the zeitgeist and distil it into a new way of being and feeling. Jack argued that it was the poet's lot, in an age of cultural crisis, to 'suffer not only *more* than others, but to suffer *for* others' in order to evolve a higher level of consciousness, 'a new co-operative enterprise of the spirit.' In reply, Judith wrote:

> I am a tranquil lake
> to mirror their joy and pain;
> and all their pain and joy
> I from my own heart make.

Their letters reveal that Judith was exhilarated and, at times, daunted by the ambitious nature of Jack's philosophical project. For the past 2000 years, Western philosophy had sought to better understand *how* we know what we know. It had been a search for general principles or underlying truths. Since then, humanity had blithely assumed that it was progressing towards greater certainty in its knowledge of the world and itself. In the 1940s, when Jack was developing and refining his thesis, Anglo-Saxon philosophy was dominated by logical positivism, a movement which rejected metaphysics and ethics as a collection of meaningless pseudo-propositions, and embraced the logic of science. Jack felt that this line of philosophy had capitulated to science as the ultimate method of inquiry and analysis. Science, particularly physics, had increased human power over, and insight into, the environment, but philosophy had failed to rise to this challenge. For all the advances in scientific knowledge, humans had not advanced their understanding of life's meaning. We now had the atom bomb but no way of dealing with the fear, the uncertainty and the sense of crisis it generated.

It was Jack's opinion that philosophy's greatest achievement so far was the recognition that our collective worldview or sense of reality is constructed through language. And because language arises only out of cooperation between individuals, it is a shared inheritance that binds people together. Modern science and philosophy had, however, atomised experience and undermined this sense of a shared reality. The result was a prevailing sense of fragmentation, alienation and meaninglessness, as reflected in the work of modernists like Samuel Beckett and T.S. Eliot. The two world wars, the destruction of the natural world and the misuse of technology were all symptoms of this 'modern psychosis': the breakdown of the old worldview. We had reached a point in history, Jack argued, where reason and intellectual analysis were failing us. According to Judith, Jack shared with Jung the view that this breakdown, at a personal level, was triggered by the undervaluing of intuitive experience. What was required was a form of emotional intelligence (although neither of them used this now popular phrase); a future in which 'the values of feeling' were prized over rationality and materialism.

In many ways, Jack's vision is only now being realised. Writing about the climate crisis, philosopher Clive Hamilton argues that a new consciousness cannot be forged purely through a scientific understanding of the world. It must come out of a different conception of reality, one that allows for 'participatory knowledge' as well as scientific knowledge. One that allows for the 'mystery of being' as well as scientific certainties. 'Such an understanding of the world requires a transformation of our attitudes, our values and our institutions; but above all it requires an expansion of ourselves.' It is the very argument that Jack was making in his philosophical writings and that Judith would continue to develop in her poetry and her essays on the environment.

Jack regarded his thesis as 'an intellectual atom bomb' that would bring about a 'revolution of thought'. He believed it was the only thing that could defeat the real A-bomb. At this time, neither Jack nor Judith believed in the political solutions on offer. To Judith, politics was 'the froth on the top of the cauldron . . . not what makes the water boil.' The important thing was to find out why the water was boiling. Jack believed that he had, and Judith was won over by his conviction and the force of his arguments. Although his ideas would never have the explosive impact he hoped for—perhaps because their time had not yet come—positive reviews in British philosophical journals of his second book, *The Structure of Modern Thought* (published by Chatto & Windus (1971) after his death) would prove his philosophical arguments to be sound.

The low sun was slanting across the park, gilding everything it touched. It was that hour of day when figures from the past might step out of the shadows, or when we feel a piercing awareness of all that has gone. Sixty years ago, Judith and Jack had sat here on this lawn, locked in passionate discussion about how philosophy might save the world. It was a strange and moving thought: the depth of their concern, the responsibility they felt, the belief that ideas and poetry could make a difference. And swirling around them would have been people like us taking their afternoon stroll, wanting nothing more than to enjoy the last rays of sunshine and to contemplate the pleasures of the night ahead.

As we headed back to Anna's house for dinner, stopping occasionally to pick up yellow-tinged frangipani flowers that had fallen on the footpath, I thought of Judith returning alone to her windowless room because propriety made it impossible for her to live with Jack. Public spaces like the park were all very well for romantic encounters when in the first flush of love but, as time passed, Jack and Judith longed for a place of their own. While they lived apart, their only shared, truly private territory was each other. Judith would later capture this in the poem 'Two Hundred Miles' in which a lover, who is separated from her beloved, imagines herself rushing back to him. Nothing else matters but seeing him 'because you are my home'.

As lovers do, they inhabited a universe of their own. The lack of recognition from the academy for Jack's ideas, combined with Judith's sensitivity to the fact that she and Jack were 'living in sin', heightened their sense of existing in a separate dimension from everyone else. There is a conspiratorial mood in their letters as they talk of how 'the world is going to obstruct us as much as it can.' But, insists Jack, 'we are going to be very happy & defy the world.' This hostile world is epitomised by the suburbs and the city itself, the world of convention and orthodox thought. In one letter Jack writes: 'We live so much on the heights that when we descend to the valley the view seems restricted.' It was a figure of speech that captured the kind of landscape both aspired to. Not only did they lack a private place where they could be intimate, but the lofty intellectual landscape they shared put them at odds with their social and physical environment.

Although they did begin negotiations for a block of land in the suburbs out of desperation for a place where Jack could devote himself to his writing without the draining demands of physical labour—the war had left him with serious heart and gastric problems—they were much more attracted by the possibility of a house on Tamborine Mountain, eighty kilometres southeast of Brisbane. Like the many artists and outsiders who have headed for the hills—the Dandenong Ranges near Melbourne, the Blue Mountains near Sydney or the Adelaide Hills—they were instinctively drawn to the natural fringe rather than the urban centre.

In Judith's mind, the city was, at best, nature tamed and trammelled. She didn't write many poems about cities—out of over four hundred poems in the *Collected Poems*, only about half a dozen refer to cities or are set in them. In these few poems, cities reek of failure, greed and fear. They are grimy and despoiled by human waste, or are sexually and intellectually sterile. Judith's growing frustration with living apart from Jack (in one letter she says 'I think we'll live and die in separate houses') and her sense that the city itself is to blame are powerful undercurrents in 'The City Asleep', which came out of this period. The poet addresses her lover who is somewhere else in the city. While the stone walls of the metropolis and the rain seem to shut them off from each other, the poet senses that 'When we are most, then we are least alone'. While physically separated, sleep joins them as they descend into mankind's storehouse of shared, primordial images: the realm of the collective unconscious.

By this time, both Judith and Jack were immersed in the writings of Carl Jung. The way the poem takes the reader back in time, beneath the stones of the city into underground catacombs, is highly reminiscent of a famous dream of Jung's in which he found himself in an old house built upon the old city wall in Basel that had many levels in it, each lower one from a more ancient period. At the very bottom was a cave or tomb filled with prehistoric pottery and bones. It was this dream that inspired Jung's idea of the collective unconscious. As well as taking us into the subterranean landscape of our shared psychic origins, the poem ends with the buried 'seed' of the individual self that 'aches and swells towards its flower of love.' The city might keep the aching lovers apart, but Judith brings them together through this journey to the 'beginning of the world'.

When Judith and Jack bought a small cottage and settled in the lush, tenebrous surrounds of Mount Tamborine, this journey continued. Here, in this conservative, rural community they would live as husband and wife even though they did not marry (because Jack's wife would not agree to a divorce) until a few years before Jack's death. Here, Meredith would be born and grow up. Here, Judith would write most of her poetry and Jack would complete his magnum opus. Although the poetry Judith would write during the next thirty years would bear the imprint of subtropical Queensland, the landscape she charted would not correlate neatly with any map. It would be as much an internal landscape as an external one. Inspired by Jack's philosophy, her fascination with Jung, the exhilaration of being in love and the primal darkness of the mountain's rainforests, her poems would dig deeper into the realms of the collective unconscious as she took her readers on a journey to 'time's own root'.

NINE

My Red Mountain

Low, smoggy cloud hovered over Brisbane the day Anna and I headed for Mount Tamborine. We took the Gold Coast freeway through outer suburbs and then turned off to the rural foothills of the Mount Tamborine plateau. 'I don't remember any of this,' Anna said, gazing out the window while I drove. She wasn't getting those flashes of deja vu that normally accompany a return to landscape from childhood. Having grown up in Brisbane, she and her parents had occasionally driven up to the mountain for day trips. Although these visits were infrequent, they made a profound impression because of the contrast between the bright summer heat of Brisbane and the wet, cool darkness of the mountain. Something about the moist darkness also made her fearful. She and her parents had walked beneath a waterfall and she had been frightened by the slippery rocks.

But nothing Anna saw now was familiar. Where were the tall, vine-tangled rainforests? Where was the mysterious, disturbing darkness? The road was climbing but there were only occasional patches of forest. Before we knew it, we were driving through a stark modern housing estate that, if not for its elevation, might have been somewhere on the fringes of Brisbane. Through a break in the trees, we saw the sea in the distance, and the tall white pillars of the Gold Coast shimmering like an ever-rising Atlantis whose satellite suburbs were now pushing into the foothills of Mount Tamborine. When Judith first arrived in Brisbane in 1943, Surfers Paradise was a small coastal town. At that time, Jack had a cottage there. Before they became lovers she would visit him with books from the university library, and would go body surfing on those long white beaches, never imagining that one day they would be overshadowed by high rise buildings. During the three decades that Judith spent on Mount Tamborine, she watched the Gold Coast swell into this sky-scraping metropolis. By the mid-1970s, she was lamenting that large portions of Tamborine were being subdivided for development. 'Already the last of the gravel red roads are being bitumened . . . And the Gold Coast approacheth closer.'

By the time we reached the top of the mountain, the vegetation was lusher and the houses and guesthouses had more established, fern-filled gardens which blended into the landscape. With its Swiss-inspired buildings and wedding-package feel, the tourist centre of Mount Tamborine reminded me of the Dandenongs. Unlike New England, which I 'knew' through the poetry, I had only vague images and expectations of Mount Tamborine before arriving here. While the New England poems capture a distinctive and recognisable terrain, the poems inspired by Mount Tamborine are different. In them, Judith would make general references to 'my red mountain' and to the rainforests, waterfalls and cliffs, the ancient ferns, flowers, vines and giant trees, the red soil, birds and native animals. Yet for all her evident delight in this new-found world, the poems don't evoke an identifiable place. The feeling I was often left with after reading them was of having entered a universal dreamscape (albeit with a subtropical flavour); of having delved into the rich compost of our psychic origins.

At the same time, the landscape of the poems—particularly those about her relationship with Jack and Meredith—is full of intimate, personal associations. For all three of them, the gardens and the rainforests of Mount Tamborine were not just emblems of their love but a living expression of it. Meredith recalls how 'the rich dark rainforest and its clambering plant world, the lush gardens and profusion of flowers, felt to me all of a piece with the strong and easy happiness that flowed between my parents and in which I bathed as my natural right.' This personal landscape and the universal dreamscape of Judith's poetry were, of course, inseparable; as are the unconscious and the collective unconscious.

Judith's deepest intuition, which shaped her whole life, was of the interconnectedness of *all* things. A sense not unlike that expressed by Wordsworth in 'Tintern Abbey': 'A motion and a spirit, that . . . rolls through all things.' But, for Judith this 'spirit' was not God in any conventional sense; it was more a form of energy. In a letter to a friend, she wrote that she had never been able to understand why we had 'divided godhead' from humanity: 'More and more I feel there isn't an "I", nor even a "we", there's an It. Oriental this may be, but it gets truer and truer for me.' Distinctions between ourselves and the external world were arbitrarily imposed by our 'dividing intellect' which alienated us from the rest of creation. As she wrote in the poem 'Rainforest':

> We with our quick dividing eyes
> measure, distinguish and are gone.
> The forest burns, the tree-frog dies,
> yet one is all and all are one.

It was no wonder Judith took to Jung, with his cosmological view of the mind, and his conviction that the gods of the 'old religions' and myths were personifications of aspects of the human psyche. 'From time immemorial,' Jung wrote, 'nature was always filled with spirit. Now, for the first time, we are living in a lifeless nature bereft of gods.' The Enlightenment might have destroyed the spirits of nature but 'not the psychic factors that correspond to them.' We most often glimpse these psychic factors in our dreams. As someone who kept a dream diary, Judith was highly attuned to this unconscious activity. She told her friend Nettie Palmer that she had particularly wild dreams when under anaesthetic, 'involving the whole of life and death and God and firmaments of screaming stars.'

In moments of great intensity, she also experienced what might be called 'waking dreams'. One evening, not long after they moved to the mountain, when she and Jack were out looking at the stars, she had a revelation of dizzying intensity. An epiphany, it would seem, inspired by the sheer exhilaration of being in love, their shared intellectual understanding of the world and the brilliance of the night sky at this elevation. It was, she would later recall, an 'almost unbearable' experience of infinitude, of 'being part of the galaxy, and of the galaxy itself being part of the consciousness of man.' In his memoir, Jung described a similar oceanic experience: 'At times I feel as if I am spread out over the landscape and inside things, and am myself living in every tree, in the splashing waves, in the clouds and the animals that come and go, in the procession of the seasons.'

Later that day we would discover the old, windy road up the mountain which wended through rainforest and bush, and which Anna recognised as the route which she took with her family on their weekend visits. Curiously, this road is called the 'new road' by the locals—even though it was laid in the 1920s—because it was the first bitumen road up the mountain from Brisbane. The road we had come by was known as the 'do-it-yourself road' because Tamborine residents had got fed up with waiting for the state government to act and had decided to build it themselves in the 1950s.

In 1953, Judith wrote a poem called 'Sanctuary' that lamented the incursion of a road through a special place full of 'antique forests and cliffs' clearly inspired by Tamborine Mountain. The poem told how, for thousands of years before the road was built, there stood an 'old gnome tree' until it was cut down by 'some axe-new boy'. This reference probably drew on a local story of the 'great grandfather Peter' macrozamia or cycad, an ancient fern-like tree which was destroyed by some young men looking for fronds to decorate a hall for a party. In the poem, regardless of a sign saying 'Sanctuary', the road sweeps ominously on, leading into 'the world's cities like a long fuse laid'.

As I got out of the car and looked around at the quaint cafes, galleries and New Age gift shops, I could almost hear the road sizzling beneath my feet.

The next day, Paul Lyons, a retired computer engineer and local historian, took me to where Jack and Judith's first house, 'Quantum', once stood. We pulled up out the front of a quarter-acre block that sat in the middle of a large farm, like an island in a sea of green. There was a very new-looking house to one side of the block and not much garden.

'This can't be the house,' I said.

'It isn't,' he said dryly. 'I helped pull theirs down.'

Ten years before, most of Quantum had burned down and the owner had asked Paul if the historical society could make use of the remaining timber. During the demolition, in a cavity between the outer weatherboards and the kitchen wall, he found the sign Quantum which Jack had carved, in raised block letters, in a solid chunk of tallowwood. The sign was now kept in the Mount Tamborine Historical Society archives.

I couldn't help feeling that Judith would have been delighted with this find, and not just because it was made by Jack and held fond memories. I think she would have also appreciated *how* it was found. Its excavation from between an inner and outer wall of the house was such a perfect metaphor for the surfacing of repressed material from the unconscious, as happens in dreams or times of crisis. The house and the life it had once contained had vanished, but this relic, which brought with it the lost world of Quantum, was a reminder of the role the unconscious plays in our conscious lives.

Growing up in New England, Judith knew all about haunted landscapes and the return of the repressed. But on Mount Tamborine, the ghosts—especially of the old forests—were more readily felt. Here, the landscape had not been so resolutely conquered and tamed, and was therefore more obviously at risk. Although my knowledge of the region's history was sketchy before I arrived, our drive up the 'do-it-yourself road' had made it quite clear how much of the mountain's past was in the process of being cleared and built over. Once you arrive at the top of the mountain, the fragments of remaining rainforest in the small National Parks at its precipitous edges serve as sad reminders of the vast subtropical forest of giant gums, red cedars, palms and vines that had once covered the Tamborine plateau. While there are few obvious traces of the Wangerriburra tribe who lived here for 40 000 years, implements such as stone axes and shaped flints are still being found. The mountain's name comes from their word 'dyambrin', which means 'place of yams'. As in New England, the Wangerriburra were driven into the less accessible regions as European settlement and land-clearing progressed.

During the walk up Long Road towards Quantum, I had noticed an old commemorative plaque on a rock that paid tribute to the early pioneers who had cleared and settled Mount Tamborine. Once the early timber-getters had exhausted the eucalypt forests of the riverflats below the plateau, they turned their sights on the less accessible rainforests of the mountain. It became a condition of ownership that the settlers must clear the land. By the time Judith and Jack arrived here in 1946, only shards of the original forests remained. They fell in love with the rainforests but sensed that most of the local inhabitants of this conservative farming community did not share their feelings. 'There was,' Judith recalled in her memoir, 'a kind of hostility still to those deep forests—since most of the descendants of the few early arrivals had spent much of their childhood and youth battling the forest for a niche on which to farm and live.'

In this hostility towards the forest, Judith also recognised a more fundamental antipathy: the age-old terror of the 'dark wood', that unknown territory on the outskirts of human settlement believed to be the haunt of evil. It is a terror, as we know from fairytales and myths, that goes back to the very origins of civilisation. Our unwillingness to confront this darkness, or to recognise that what lurks in this wood is a projection of our own demons, preoccupies many of her early Mount Tamborine poems.

Now, as I surveyed the block where Quantum once stood, I tried to imagine the house based on what I'd read and seen in photographs: a simple two-roomed, timber-getter's hut made of 'reject weatherboards that never quite met' with a front veranda hung with local ferns. The neighbours had told them the cottage wasn't fit to live in, but Judith and Jack were perfectly contented with it.

A sense of what the community and the house itself were like when they first arrived here can be gleaned from a dream Judith had twenty years later. It was a dream about moving into a 'primitive' old house on the 'shelf' of a mountain, which she recognised as Tamborine. Clearly inspired by Quantum as they first found it, this dream house was 'very dirty, its cupboards knocked together out of old slabs.' The local people, who were 'very Puritan, very regional', belonged to a settlement of survivors from an old mining town which had closed down long ago. Its location on a 'shelf' symbolised its sense of isolation and its desire to remain on the edge of things, locked in the past. In the dream, Judith wondered how she and Jack would get along with the locals and felt that they had better watch their tongues. However, the people turned out to be friendly and told them the story of the house, which they claimed was haunted.

This aspect of the dream—the belief that the house was haunted—was evidently inspired by the locals' opinion that the house was not fit to live in. Her dream treats this claim as a projection of the community's state of mind, for it is *they* who are haunted or possessed by the past. As Jung argues: 'Since nobody is capable of recognising just where and how much he himself is possessed and unconscious, he simply projects his own condition upon his neighbour.'

Judith channelled this early impression of Mount Tamborine into her poem 'Camphor Laurel', which she wrote while living at Quantum. In it, a haunted house laments that things are 'not like the old days'. The house is the collective psyche of the local community, while the 'old days' are represented by a group of colourful frontier figures who are buried underneath it. Connecting past and present, conscious and unconscious, is the sweet-smelling camphor laurel tree in the backyard whose roots go deep under the house, breaking the old bones and splitting the house's foundations. The tree is a kind of Yggdrasil, the tree of life in Scandinavian mythology (which Judith was reading about at the time) that unites heaven, earth and hell, and represents life, knowledge, time and space. In this poem, it illustrates how the collective unconscious and the collective experiences of all humanity inform and unsettle individual lives.

It was Jung's belief that we are all in the grip of unconscious psychic forces, both creative and destructive, of which we have little comprehension. Before the Age of Enlightenment—the eighteenth century philosophical movement characterised by rationalism—the workings of the unconscious were given expression through myths and religion. A recognition of the divine as part of ordinary life not only helped people make sense of the world, but also gave shape to the mysterious workings of the mind, allowing individuals to deal with their inner conflicts. The Enlightenment, however, fostered the conviction that reason was the only path to truth, and so laid the foundations for modern secular society. Jung argued that by privileging the rational above the non-rational, and by repressing or denying the dark side of human nature, we create a violent 'shadow', a time-bomb waiting to go off. He believed that in times of great social uncertainty—as rocked Germany in the 1930s and led to the Second World War—this collective psychosis erupts through the veneer of civilisation, with nations projecting the darkness within themselves on to their enemies.

In the aftermath of this horrific war, Judith began applying Jung's thinking quite literally to her own backyard. The haunted house is a classic symbol of a psyche unsettled by past trauma. As she delved deeper into the world of Mount Tamborine and its rainforests, Judith would find even more fertile material for her quest to explore the ways in which we are haunted by our collective history, and of the need to confront this darkness if we are to save ourselves and the planet.

TEN

In the Dark Wood

Over the hill behind Quantum is the source of Cedar Creek, a small spring which becomes Curtis Falls a few kilometres downstream and then flows on into the torrential Cedar Creek waterfall at Cedar Creek National Park, further down the mountain. It is not easy to find the exact location of the source because it shifts with the rising and lowering of the watertable. Local historian, Paul Lyons, took me to a spot near a dead-end road and pointed to a small pond made inaccessible by its swampy surrounds, tangled bush and long grasses. The source, he said, lay somewhere between this spot and the next road. Less than a kilometre away is a protected grove of cycads, fern-like 'dinosaur' trees which have existed for almost three hundred million years.

The idea of finding a 'source'—of life, of inspiration—is enormously seductive for a poet, especially a poet like Judith for whom the landscape was inseparable from the topography of the human mind. So, when Judith and Jack went walking one day in search of the source of Cedar Creek—as told in her poem 'The Ancestors'—they were not simply following the stream through 'the sunny grass so clear' up to the source of the creek. They were embarking on a kind of quest, travelling back in time to the deep past which still haunts humanity in the form of unconscious drives and irrational impulses; back to our psychic and physical origins.

The poem describes the growing darkness in a patch of forest where there stood 'fern-trees locked in endless age'. In the trunks of these ferns 'shaggy as an ape', Judith sensed the 'dark bent foetus' of our ancestors. The poem records the sudden intuition of what it means to carry all this prehistory—'the old ape-knowledge of the embryo'— within oneself; how it lives on in the present and connects us all.

> Their silent sleep is gathered round the spring
> that feeds the living, thousand-lighted stream
> up which we toiled into this timeless dream.

Just as the body bears traces of its various evolutionary stages, says Jung, so too does the psyche. Judith described this compressed history as 'the road from protoplasm to man'. Her intense efforts to comprehend the stages of this road and the vast amount of experience and knowledge gained along the way are captured in one of her dreams. She dreamed she was a piece of protoplasm, 'knowing in a dreadful way that I had to pass through eons and eons of learning and growing and changing all the way up to a human.'

Anna and I had gone only a few steps down the steep path into the Palm Grove forest—the section of National Park closest to Quantum— when I began to see why the darkness made such an impression on Judith. Outside it was a bright, sunny afternoon. But here, it was as if we had entered a tunnel. In this shadowy green-room, only small patches of sunlight penetrated the dense canopy of twisted vines, piccabean palms and towering strangler figs. It had rained the night before and a rich, damp smell rose from the earth.

In the upper storey of the forest we could hear the thick drone of bees, a sound which was later overtaken by the reverberating metallic chant of cicadas until the air itself seemed to hum. The elongated call and snapped-wire answer of whip birds pinged above our heads. Fallen palm fronds, branches and leaves made the ground crackle as we walked. Such was the obvious fecundity of the whole place that you could almost see things growing and rotting before your eyes.

The zig-zagging path was narrow and more overgrown than sections of the National Park closer to the township. For the first time, I felt I was glimpsing what the whole plateau might have been like before settlement.

One of the early, and unusually enlightened, settlers on Mount Tamborine wrote in his journal:

Those who see the Mountain today have no idea what the original Tamborine Mountain looked like, nor do they know of the teeming wildlife that was here awaiting destruction by the white man's axe . . . I did my share with axe and fire. Many times have I thought about it as I have moved over the ground where the big trees stood. Do I owe this destroyed wildlife a debt? Perhaps I do?

It was Judith's belief that we all owe the destroyed wildlife more of a debt than we can ever imagine—and not only because of the loss of a rich and ancient ecosystem. As human animals, our minds bear the imprint of the wilderness out of which we arose. We might think we have left it behind as we huddle behind the walls of civilisation but the wilderness is still in us. Only when we are able to acknowledge and accept this inheritance will the pattern of destruction end. This means acknowledging the limitations of reason.

As literary critic Terry Eagleton puts it: 'It is only if reason can draw upon energies and resources deeper, more tenacious, and less fragile than itself that it is capable of prevailing.' While hard to define, these 'deeper resources' are elements of our psychological makeup and evolutionary history that we have repressed or undervalued in the post-Enlightenment world. For Judith, these 'deeper resources' lay, above all, in our emotional connection with the natural world. As a Jungian, she believed that we are fundamentally driven by impulses, feelings and sensations. But we have failed to recognise this, having prized rationality above all. An emotional response to nature is as valid, she argued, as a scientific one: the pleasure we take in a sunny day on a spring morning is as 'real' as a barometer reading. This is why, Judith argues, long held attitudes to exploitation cannot be altered by rational argument or threats alone. 'Our feelings and emotions must be engaged and engaged on a large scale. Whether scientists like it or not, it is *feeling* that sways public opinion, far more than reason; it is feeling that spurs us to protest.'

Decades after her arrival on Mount Tamborine, her practical experience as a conservationist would reinforce her early intuition that what was needed was 'not only rational recognition of the problem but human concern, distress and love.' She knew that many National Parks in Australia had been founded because ordinary people (such as her father) were moved by deep feeling for these places. She also sensed that literature could play a vital role in rousing these feelings. The Romantic poets had, after all, helped change the way we understand our relationship with nature—and in very practical ways. The change in consciousness brought about by the poetry of William Wordsworth, argues literary critic Jonathan Bates, ultimately led to the establishment of National Parks in the United States and later in the United Kingdom.

As we walked deeper into Palm Grove, it struck me that Judith's early Tamborine poems were just as driven by a desire to change people's minds and behaviour as were her later, more outspoken and obviously political works. But rather than focusing on broad social and environmental issues, these introspective poems conduct their own therapy—the underlying assumption being that political change begins with the individual. As she would later write: 'We must regenerate ourselves if we are to regenerate the earth.' These early poems challenge readers to confront the workings of their psyches, to explore the forest inside their heads and to own the many conflicting forces that lurk there. Like Virgil leading Dante through his 'gloomy wood', Judith becomes our tour guide through the circles of the unconscious. Look at this cycad, she says to us, in the poem of that name. It is a living symbol of the beginnings of time, of your origins, of that which remains unchanged within you despite the passage of millennia.

> Take their cold seed and set it in the mind,
> and its slow root will lengthen deep and deep
> till, following, you cling on the last ledge
> over the unthinkable, unfathomed edge
> beyond which man remembers only sleep.

Think on it, our guide urges, and let it take you back to a time when your ancestors lived like these plants, unconscious of their existence yet completely at one with their world. You ask what the unconscious is? It is that primal part of yourself you have forgotten.

Other poems, such as 'The Forest Path', recall a journey down a path similar to the one that Anna and I were now on. As the walkers move away from the security of civilisation and into the claustrophobic world of the forest, they find themselves growing ever more afraid. Not so much of getting lost, as of the loss of self.

They turn to speak to their friends only to find they have become the trunks of overgrown trees. Snakes begin to uncoil from their own 'hollow hearts'. Confronted with their own insecurity and with the primeval depths of the psyche, the walkers can only recoil. As tour guide, Judith is showing us how repression works. How we turn our backs on such visions and dismiss them as waking nightmares or panic-fuelled figments of the imagination. Or how we project them on to the forest itself.

Ironically enough, a mild form of the anxiety that marks 'The Forest Path' did overtake us. I had once been attacked by a man as I walked along a semi-secluded suburban lane. As a consequence, I was easily unnerved whenever alone, or with another woman, in a place that was isolated or off the beaten track. For her own reasons, Anna shared my fears. When we had walked through the Curtis Falls park near the township, there had been noisy school children and other groups. But here, there was no one else. No bustle of human traffic to make us feel secure. Just the whip birds, and the alarming scuffle of brush turkeys suddenly bursting out of the undergrowth and on to the path. Although we pressed on, neither of us could relax.

In 'The Forest Path', Judith tells us that if terror had not overtaken us, we might have discovered that this path did not lead to death but to a new way of being. What this 'birth' of a new understanding might mean is made more explicit in a letter she wrote to some university students who asked her about the political implications of the nascent conservation movement in 1971. Signs of a change of attitudes and values were apparent, she replied, in the emerging discipline of ecology. The fact that 'we are beginning to recognise that we are not separate from what we have called "nature", indicates a way forward.'

For a short time, we pushed on. Through gaps in the foliage came flashes of sheer, rocky cliffs that fell away to the hinterland of the

Gold Coast far below. Almost all of the Tamborine National Parks are perched on the precipitous edges of the plateau because this land was difficult for timber-getters to reach and no good for farming—hence its preservation as National Park. I had wanted to do the Jenyns Falls circuit, which followed these cliff edges, but the path was closed because of landslides. The park literature described the terrain as 'geologically unstable' and therefore unsafe. I knew there were times, after flooding, when chunks of roads on the mountain used to fall away. One Mother's Day, Meredith skipped Sunday school, and she and her mother went walking in Palm Grove. It was, Judith recalled, 'one of the mountain's extra special days with cloud-shadows and greeny-blue forests and we went into the deep scrub and drank from a little spring and found new sorts of funguses and birds.' Idyllic it might have been, but at one stage Meredith blithely set off down a path that had collapsed from a landslide. Judith had to pull her back with 'grazed elbow and a thorn in her foot'.

Clearly landslides were a real danger, but I couldn't help wondering if there was another reason why the Jenyns Falls circuit had been closed. Just as it is never reported how often people jump from the Sydney Harbour Bridge, so too do we rarely hear about the number of people who go to National Parks to end their lives. Raymond Curtis, a descendent of a settler family who had worked in the Tamborine National Parks for many years, told me that it was not an uncommon occurrence. I also knew of someone who had chosen the freezing high planes of the Victorian Alps in which to lie down and not wake up.

Even if the path to Jenyns Falls had not been closed, I suspect that Anna and I would not have gone there. Our anxieties would have held us back. Yet in my mind, I had already walked it. Each time I'd read the poem 'The Precipice', I had seen the 'dark of the mountain forest opened like flesh' as a woman, clutching her children's hands, ran along the path we were on, 'possessed and intent as any lover'. The story which inspired the poem was a true one. The woman's husband, a soldier traumatised by his experiences during the Second World War, had become violent. Unable to bear his abuse, or the prospect of nuclear conflict which loomed large in the 1950s, the woman took her children and caught a bus up the mountain 'behaving like any woman, but she was no longer living.' When the woman and her children didn't return from their walk, search parties went out to look for them. The searchers eventually came across a trail of lolly papers on the Jenyns Falls path. In the poem, Judith imagined the woman at the edge of the cliff, taking the children in her arms 'because she loved them'. Then she jumped, 'parting the leaves and the night's curtain.'

This is one of a number of poems that register the apocalyptic mood of the Cold War; it also faintly echoes 'Nigger's Leap, New England'. Both events, as told in the poems, happen at night. Both concern the havoc wreaked by the dark side of the human psyche. Both are about being driven into the abyss. Only in this case, the woman chose her own end (and that of her children) rather than face threats beyond her control. Remembering the vertiginous pull of the cliffs at Point Lookout, I felt quietly relieved that Jenyns Falls was closed and that I was off the hook.

We decided to turn back. We had experienced enough to know that the real threat did not come from the forest. As we climbed back up the steep path and out into the sunshine, I could still hear the ricocheting sound of whip birds calling to each other, as if announcing that the danger had passed. The humans were gone.

ELEVEN

Beyond the Burning Wind

About a kilometre down Long Road from Quantum, we found the house that Judith and Jack bought in 1951. It was their home until Jack's death in 1966, after which Judith lived there alone for almost another ten years.

> We were fortunate, house; in a world of exiles
> stateless, homeless wandering, spying, murdering,
> wars, bewilderments, losses and betrayals,
> we found each other.
> In your spaces and awkward corners
> we spread our lives out, fitted and grew together.

This part of Long Road was more settled than the rural end around Quantum. With the vogue for mountain weddings, a number of places had been turned into reception centres for weddings with mythical names like 'Avalon'. Judith named their house 'Calanthe' after the local native orchid, *Calanthe veratrifolia*, known as the Flying Dove.

But it was not called Calanthe any more. Like the wedding reception venues, its new name harked nostalgically back to Arthurian legend.

The tall tecoma hedge that once grew at the front had been replaced by a wrought-iron fence and high, forbidding gate with cameos of mysterious-looking intertwined snakes—all of which looked too grand for the modest weatherboard beyond the iron bars. There was something spooky about this gate, especially the snake symbols. In Judith's poem 'Habitat'—a meditation on the experience of living in this house—she refers to a dream in which 'Heraldic animals / stand at the garden entrance. / My snakes are at home there.' (A carpet snake used to live in their ceiling.) Either the current owners had read Judith's poem and made the dream come true, so to speak, or Judith had foreseen it.

The owners had told me they would be away, and I knew we would be trespassing if we went in, but I couldn't help feeling we had a right to be here. This garden had been Judith's handiwork and her refuge. Everything I knew about it made me feel possessive towards it, as if it were one of her poems. Peering through the gate, I thought of the barriers our minds erect around poetry. Why, I wondered, are we so intimidated by these small plots of words? And why do we feel as if we are trespassing when we try to approach them? A number of friends had told me that they would like to read Judith's poetry but didn't know how to find a way in. They felt they needed a key.

At first it looked as though the gate was locked but, with a bit of jiggling, the stiff latch loosened. Hesitantly, we pushed it open and walked up the gravel path. Although the house had been renovated and gentrified, the row of prehistoric-looking cycads that used to brush against the front window panes were still there, giving me hope that the lineaments of Judith's garden would also remain. I knocked on the front door and waited, just to check. When no one answered, we took the side path into the deep backyard that sloped down towards a paddock where cattle grazed.

When Judith, Jack and Meredith first moved here, the garden had been a jungle of kikuyu grass. Over a period of twenty years, Judith spent thousands of hours pouring her energy and love into this plot of earth. Early on, she found remnants in the soil of the first settlers on the mountain—bits of crockery, smashed bottles, iron bolts, lost toys. Maintaining the garden was a constant battle with the elements— cyclones, hail storms, drought—and with the extraordinarily rapid rate of growth in the subtropics. There were few natives at first, except for the cycads and the calanthe orchid their neighbour had procured from a block of private rainforest. Judith would come to regard these white flower sprays that grew up to five feet high as 'one of the glories' of the rainforest. Yet a domestic garden is, in so many ways, the antithesis of a rainforest. It is ordered, trimmed and tended: nature made manageable. Although she would later set about turning the garden into a miniature rainforest, in the early 1950s the traditional European garden was still the prevailing model for what a garden should be.

Like so many Australian gardens, it was now a jumble of past and present trends, of native and introduced plants, of rainforest and European trees. Alongside the eucalypts, paperbarks, bottle brush— all of which were planted by Judith—were azaleas, oak trees, pencil pines and avocadoes.

Much of the backyard had a rambling and semi-wild atmosphere which the owners were attempting to put in order. I passed a half-built, geometric garden bed of raw red earth with edges of interlocking circles made from brick. Beyond it, where I suspected Judith's vegetable garden had once been, was a newly created rose garden divided into four parts by gravel walkways, with a wrought-iron sculpture at the centre based on the same Arthurian symbol as found on the gate. The whole arrangement made me think of a crematorium. Only the plaques were missing.

I sat down on a bench overlooking the yard. All these changes raised a disturbing question: to what extent was this still the garden that Judith had made? My experience of the gardens at Wallamumbi and Wongwibinda had shown me the folly of hoping to step into a perfectly preserved past. But Calanthe was different from the New England gardens: those gardens had not been Judith's creations (apart from the tiny garden of native violets she made when her mother was ill). What remained of Judith's garden here at Calanthe mattered because it was her creation, the product of her labour and her imagination, a kind of living poem.

It occurred to me that this was what I had been foolishly hoping for—the experience of stepping into one of her poems. A poem in which you could smell the flowers. A poem alive with insects and birds, as well as plants. A poem full of colour and light and textures that afforded what Judith's work was always straining towards: a direct and unmediated communion with nature. As a child, her parents had read to her from Robert Louis Stevenson's *A Child's Garden of Verses*. And in a letter to a friend, she once described poetry as a 'garden to wander in'. If this was so, then the reverse should also be true. Which was why these newly built garden beds were so unnerving. The garden, as it now stood, was like one of her poems with crossings-out and new words written in by a stranger's hand.

The truth I was resisting was that, while a poem is a finished artefact, a garden is always a work-in-progress. Judith knew very well that the perfect garden in her mind's eye could never be realised—although it did not stop her from trying. This imaginary garden drew heavily on her memories of the past, especially the 'lost garden' of her youth. So strong was this attachment that she cultivated certain plants which reminded her of Wallamumbi. She was delighted when the wild violets—the flower she had planted and nurtured during her mother's illness—thrived. She told a friend that she had always wanted a lawn that would have dew and shadows and plenty of spiders. 'It rejoices me to have one now,' she wrote, foreshadowing her poem 'Reminiscence': 'I was born into a coloured country; / spider-webs in dew on feathered grass'. Another letter described how the garden was 'full of violets, wattle, and daffodils just coming out. I'll put in a bit of my pennyroyal . . . It reminds me of mustering cattle on hills covered with it, the smell behind the mob was mingled cow and pennyroyal.'

Judith had grown up in an environment in which man actively shaped the land. She did not condone what her pastoralist family did to the forests that once covered much of New England. But she had retained this hands-on relationship with the land; she needed to get her fingers into the soil. Poetry was a genteel pursuit she associated with her mother and life inside the house. As a girl, she had always identified strongly with what she called Outside: 'My childhood is divided, in my mind, between the problems of Inside and the freedoms of Outside.' Outside was the world of the garden and beyond. It was the male domain of mustering and running the property, of taking control of one's fate. She could see the folly of humans trying to impose their will on the wider landscape—especially when it damaged the environment—but it took her much longer to let go of the desire to leave her stamp on her own private landscape. Only when she was living at Edge, where nature was not so amenable to the foreign aesthetic of the European garden, would she finally let go of this dream.

I dug the tip of my shoe into the soft, rust red earth. For a moment, I was tempted to reach down and take a handful, it looked so rich and edible. I thought of how Judith sometimes worked on poems in her head as she did the gardening. And how deeply satisfying it would have been to combine the head, heart and body in these simultaneous creative acts. At times, she must have felt she were conjuring poems out of the earth itself. This intense identification with the soil as the source of life and creativity is most evident in her early poems which celebrate the poet's power as godlike creator. With their garden imagery, they bring to mind God presiding over the creation of Eden. The crucial difference being that the poet is not above or separate from her creation. In 'The Maker', her position is more akin to a gardener than to God as she takes 'all living things that are', cultivates them and lovingly transforms them.

> I hold the crimson fruit
> and plumage of the palm;
> flame-tree, that scarlet spirit,
> in my soil takes root.

In 'Woman to Child', this earthy imagery is taken a step further. The soil not only represents the poet's imagination but also the mother's womb: 'I am the earth, I am the root, / I am the stem that fed the fruit, / the link that joins you to the night,' says the mother to her unborn child. The poem—written before Judith became a mother herself—celebrates birth on many levels: the birth of a child, the birth of a poem and the birth of a new self for a new world order, all of which are contained in the image of a seed pushing up through the soil.

A garden, by definition, is a piece of land that bears the imprint of human design. In a similar way, these poems are born of a fusion of the imagination with the natural world. Talking about how raw experience becomes art, Judith once wrote: 'What cooks out of sight in the basement comes up as a meal. I may well have picked it from the vegetable garden but I don't always know it when it reappears.' This rich red soil beneath my feet was her constant reminder of that mysterious cycle, and of how all forms of creation begin with the 'living earth'.

Once she became a mother, Judith's identification with her garden took on greater urgency. The garden was no longer purely a vehicle for creative expression or a way of communing with nature, but also a safe haven for her child. After Meredith's birth, Judith knew what it meant to be 'overmastered by life' and to confront the terror that came with it. The poems that came out of this experience register humility in the face of the overwhelming natural forces that govern childbirth. Rather than boldly asserting the poet's creative power, they pledge a mother's unconditional love and desire to protect her child. As the mother says to her child in 'The Watcher': 'I am the garden beyond the burning wind'.

After an ectopic pregnancy almost killed her five years later, Judith adopted a stiff upper lip when reporting what had happened. Yet the experience clearly shook her and the knowledge that she couldn't have any more children left her sad and feeling suddenly old. One day, while in the garden chasing some of their cows to the creek for water, she came across an old blown-down pear tree which was still managing to put out a few blossoms even though it could not bear fruit. In it, she found a symbol for her own condition. She wrote a poem in her head and called it 'Old Woman's Song', and took it back to the house with her, along with a branch of the blossoms.

Even behind a thin veil of cloud, the midday sun was painfully glary. In this almost fluorescent light, the garden—with its half-finished landscaping—looked bedraggled and blanched. Anna told me that many nurseries in Brisbane were going out of business because of the drought. While Judith, too, had to contend with hailstorms, cyclones and drought, the lasting impression from her letters is of a garden full of flowers, exuberant growth and a veggie patch bursting with edible delights. In one letter, she describes herself as 'purring' her way around the garden. In another, she ecstatically reports that 'the garden is rather a dream'.

Only scraps of that dream were left now. I looked blindly around at the trees and plants wondering which were old enough to have been here in Judith's day. Things grew so fast in the subtropics it was hard to know. And many of these plants were unfamiliar to me. Anna pointed out some wild ginger growing under a gnarled, old-looking flowering tree, along with some ferns and orchids. It was probably a fragment of the miniature rainforest Judith had tried to create. I knew the names she mentioned in her letters—cunjevoi, flame-trees, kunzea—but had no idea what they looked like.

Feeling vaguely at a loss, I wandered down to the very bottom where a shadowy copse of large, richly foliaged trees hinted at other worlds. As a child, Judith had loved the thought of her garden coming alive with elves, fairies and goblins under the cover of darkness. Even as an adult, she had been drawn to the garden at night. I might not be able to experience the 'living poem' Judith had created, but in this shadowy spot I could begin to imagine what it might have *felt* like. In the darkness, the literal details no longer mattered. The fenced-in world of the garden took on an infinite quality at night. The stars became the garden's flowers transplanted into the sky, or a 'swarm of honey bees' in a great field. When Meredith was old enough, they regularly went out into the garden to identify the stars. (The mountain remains a mecca for star-gazers and has few street lights in order not to dull the full splendour of the night sky.) In that dazzling garden in the sky, Judith found a record of human history and our relationship with the cosmos. With its various mythic formations based on the zodiac—archetypes from the unconscious—she saw the night sky as the human psyche writ-large.

This vast, 'unconscious' darkness looms large in her poetry. She often wrote late at night when Jack and Meredith were asleep and the household chores were done: 'Darkness where I find my sight.'

After Jack's death, when Meredith had left home and the house was so silent it woke her, she would sometimes go out into the garden and lie on a mattress to watch the stars. I could imagine her fixing on Venus's 'clear, sad light' and recalling the poem she had written about it. How modern man has, in the 'neon night', forgotten the 'ritual phases of love'. With Jack gone, she would have felt more sharply than ever the pain of this loss: this 'hellfire blaze of the heart'.

There were times, though, when the 'towering universe' beyond her lighted room was too disturbingly infinite and impersonal for contemplation, and she would turn her mind instead to the achievements of man. Yet, as she grew more disillusioned by the extent of our pollution of the earth, even the vastness of the night sky began to seem contaminated, and humankind's achievements less golden. One poem tells of waking from a dream to see what looked like a meteorite blazing through the night sky. Or was it, she asks herself, 'some sad man-wrought metal?'

During her first decade at Calanthe, Judith was absorbed by the world of her garden, motherhood and writing—along with the constant struggle to make ends meet. Being reserved, hard of hearing and introspective, her natural inclination was to keep to herself. In the early 1940s, when she was asked to be on the committee for the Queensland Authors' and Artists' Association, she had recoiled from the idea. She wondered if she *ought* to do it but clearly didn't want to. 'I've got no sense of public service whatever,' she told Jack. It's a remarkable statement given her outspoken public activism later in life, and an indication of the transformation she underwent as her commitment to environmentalism deepened.

As tempting as it must have been to withdraw behind the high tecoma hedge, it was not in Judith's make-up to turn her back on the wider world. The garden was, after all, the place where the seeds of her environmentalism had been sown when she was a child. Throughout the 1950s, her poetry continued to shine a spotlight on the darker corners of the psyche. But by the mid-fifties, she was also beginning to write poems like 'Sanctuary' and 'At Cooloolah', which are more explicit in their condemnation of our impact on the natural world and of white Australians' complicity in the extermination of the indigenous peoples. Her friendship with wildflower artist and naturalist, Kathleen McArthur, helped focus her growing anxiety about the destruction of the natural environment she saw during family camping trips in Queensland. As yet, there was no environmental movement, just individuals and small groups of conservationists who had to contend with the triumphal, post-war rhetoric of nation building—'conquering', 'taming' and 'transforming'—words which sanctioned the bulldozing of the countryside on an unprecedented scale.

Judith's changing awareness was reflected in her garden as she began to plant more natives. The name she had given to the house was a clear sign of her attachment to native flowers and this became more pronounced as her friendship with Kathleen deepened. They would go 'wildflowering' together near Caloundra, where Kathleen lived, and further north on the Noosa Plains. Meredith remembers the endless walks they went on when she was a girl, and of Kathleen bounding ahead to identify vast carpets of flowers. Meredith and Judith would also pick wildflowers from the eastern edge of the mountain and make them into colourful bunches, which they entered in the Best Wild Flowers section of the local flower show. They always won because no one else was interested in native flowers.

For all her dreams of cultivating a perfect garden, Judith knew that a gardener's desire for control over nature is ultimately futile and fraught with pitfalls. In 'That Seed', the poet tells how she took a red fruit from a rainforest tree and tried to cultivate it. When nothing came of it, she threw the soil into the garden. Where it fell, 'quite against my plan', sprang up a tree that grew 'as tall as a man'. Too close to the house, it would, in time, shade the windowsill, beat its branches against the wall and even smash the roof if it fell in a storm. In this way, the poem rebukes the gardener's delusions of godlike control. But the inescapable truth is that the gardener still has the final say. This is, the poem reminds us, the moral dilemma that we all must face, both in our own backyards and in the wider world: 'Shall I take an axe to it / or shall I let it grow?'

It is not surprising, then, that the crucial shift Judith made from private poet to public activist during her years on Mount Tamborine first registered as concern for the welfare of her own 'backyard'. She complained to her good friend Barbara Blackman that 'down the creek the chain-saw keeps on whining and trees fall with a crash . . . The big scrub up near the cemetery is a desert of ashes and stumps.' Changes were afoot in her local community that she could not ignore.

In the early 1960s, Judith joined the conservation subcommittee of the local Progress Association. While most of the inhabitants of Mount Tamborine were politically conservative and supported development, Judith found a small group who shared her concerns. The committee did a lot of work with local schools, educating students about conservation, and holding competitions and outings.

Once Meredith started boarding school in Brisbane in 1962, Judith's attention turned outward beyond the mountain. In that year, she helped found the Wildlife Preservation Society of Queensland, which began publishing the magazine *Wildlife*. Like the conservation subcommittee in Tamborine, the society aimed to educate people about the need to preserve the natural environment. In time, the achievements of this small but growing group would be monumental. In the face of powerful opposition from the state government and big business interests, their efforts would eventually bring about the National Parks of Cooloola, the Great Barrier Reef and Fraser Island.

In many ways, Judith's focus was still on her 'backyard'. It was just that her sense of what constituted her backyard had expanded. Cooloola and the Great Barrier Reef were part of her 'other' backyard at Boreen Point, just north of Noosa, where she and Jack had bought a holiday shack in the 1950s.

TWELVE

Eye of the Earth

There was a strange feeling of pressure building, of being squeezed through a narrow opening into a confined space as we drove into Noosa. I realised why when I looked at a map: the town is wedged in-between the Noosa River, the headland and Lake Weyba, the lowest of the chain of lakes in the Noosa River system. On the one hand, development is curbed by these natural features. On the other, the town's location makes for relatively high density in a small area. The crowds restlessly surging along on the shopping strip behind the main beach left me with a sinking feeling about what changes I might find at Boreen Point, which had been a sleepy backwater when Judith knew it.

Yet in the National Park on the headland, amongst the banksias and pandanus palms, it was tranquil and crowd-free. At the rocky chasm of Hell's Gate, we watched a school of dolphins swimming by. In the bright sunshine, the sea was divided into two distinct bands of colour, as if a line had been drawn across it. Close in, the water was clear aquamarine. On the other side of the line, the dark blue was so abrupt it made me shiver. 'No one has marked the sea,' Judith once wrote. Remembering the murky trails of effluent and litter I had seen drifting off-shore at various beaches in Europe, I wished it were true. As we walked back, we could see Laguna Bay and the beach of Coloured Sands in the distance, reaching all the way to Fraser Island at its northern-most tip. And somewhere behind the scrub-covered dunes of this vast stretch of sand lay Lake Cootharaba and Boreen Point.

Clear of Tewantin—once a town and now a suburban extension of Noosa—the countryside opened out into farmland and state forest. Half an hour later we took the Boreen Point turn-off and drove straight into a time-warp. Only twenty kilometres from Noosa, and yet a world away. Judith, Jack and Meredith first came up this way in the mid-1950s with Judith's friend Kathleen McArthur, who had invited them to go looking for wildflowers on the sand-plains north of Noosa. In Judith's day, there were no street names or even proper streets at Boreen, just sandy tracks between nine or ten houses 'delectably perched on a lake shore above a pink and white sandstone cliff.'

In letters written in the first rush of excitement after buying their holiday shack, she rhapsodises about the 'wild and birdy lakes, lost in the wallum country; bordered by paperbarks grown old and twisty and little white sand beaches with reeds and fishing herons, and wildflower swamps and trees.' There were now a dozen streets and a population of three hundred, but the essence of the place seemed unchanged. A small, bush-covered bluff nosing into a lake so vast it made the land feel no more substantial than a mirage. In Judith's writing, Boreen Point was a place defined by shimmering reflections:

All day the candid staring of the lake
holds what's passing and forgets the past.

Unlike Noosa, it had no buzzing shopping hub, just a cafe-cum-real estate agency and a general store down by the lake. If there was a hub at all, it was the lake itself.

As we drove down towards it, I strained to see the water through the foreshore trees. I imagined it as a mirror of the sky: a picture of timeless serenity and a perfect place for contemplation. In Judith's memory and in her writing, Lake Cootharaba was always blue—'blue as a doll's eye'—and the small sandy beaches were glittering white. But what greeted us suggested that neither was the case any more, if it had ever been. Driven by a gusty wind, small catamarans skimmed across an expanse of murky brown water, while other yachts lay beached on beige-coloured sand.

'Blue as a doll's eye?' Anna laughed.

'It's probably the wind, churning it up,' I said, not knowing what to think. I watched the yachts leaping over the small brown waves. It was hard to imagine this tea-coloured water ever looking blue. We struck up a conversation with a weathered-looking sailor, and asked him about it. On sunny mornings, if the water was still, he said, the lake *could* look blue. But he seemed to think it was stretching things. 'Lots of people don't come here because they think the lake's dirty. But it's just clay from the lake bottom mixed up with the sand.' We agreed it might be a blessing, if it kept the crowds away. Each morning during our stay, I would go to the kitchen window of our rented house to see if the lake had turned blue.

One of the things Judith most loved about their shack was its view of the lake. In her memoir, she recalled how 'in that little, light-filled concrete house I suffered through a failed pregnancy that nearly killed me, Jack through a bout of flu that almost turned into pneumonia . . . but the house remained solid, warm and comforting and the blues of the lake shone through its windows.' That view was now blocked by a two-storey brick house a few doors down. But their house remained largely untouched: a quaint little cottage with a rough, white-washed facade, a concrete porch and the name 'Melaleuca'—in Jack's copperplate—still there on the front wall.

That evening, we walked by the lake amongst luminous paperbarks with their arthritic branches and knotted roots clutching at the rocky shore. I knew that the lake was a haven for bird-life, and that a number of Judith's poems from her collection *Birds* were inspired by what she saw here. While these often whimsical poems were written to appeal to children, they are as concerned with the way we construct nature as are her more 'serious' poems. We had seen some pelicans earlier on, gathered on a small sandbar, having a conference. There was something wonderfully comic about the way they were crammed together, as if afraid of getting their feet wet. In her poem about pelicans, Judith acknowledges this comic element: 'that old clever Noah's Ark . . . kind as an ambulance-driver'. But at the same time, she makes it clear that our indulgent response is a form of evasion. We prefer these birds to spiders and snakes because we can project comforting human qualities on to them. They allow us an 'easy faith' in nature and ourselves.

This warning note sounds throughout much of her later poetry. While the early Mount Tamborine poems pluck symbols from her garden and the rainforest to represent the creative and destructive impulses within the human psyche, Judith grew increasingly uneasy about treating nature as 'forest of symbols for poetic harvesting'. As a girl she had dreamed of learning the 'Master-Words', of being able to give voice to the heard and unheard murmurings of the natural world. Yet more than ever she was conscious that 'Words are not meanings for a tree' and that nature's own language would always elude her. She might hear 'one strange word' in the bubbling of a mountain spring, but would never know the translation. She might find tantalising scribbles on the trunk of a gum but could not decipher them. The lake brought this home to her more sharply than almost anything else because it was poetry in its purest form.

In her early poem 'The Maker', she had boldly announced that 'I am a tranquil lake / to mirror their joy and pain'. It was every artist's impossible dream: to be able to take into oneself 'all living things that are' and reflect them back in all their complexity for the world to appreciate and understand. Twelve years on, the real Lake Cootharaba forced Judith to confront the narcissism of this presumption. As nature's poetry, the real lake reflects back everything that crosses its path—stars, sky, clouds, trees—but also captures life's endless, moment-by-moment flux in a way that a man-made artefact can never do. 'Eye of the earth,' she says to the lake, 'my meaning's what you are.' The lake is, quite literally, the poem Judith dreams of writing, except that she can only do it through language. When she casts the 'net' of her mind out over the lake, she can only draw in words. Everything else drains through the holes in the net, and slips her grasp. No poem can capture reality as does the reflection in a lake. In the end, Judith concludes as much. When she looks into the lake, she sees herself. Underlying the poem is the fear that we can never be true to nature. What we see in it will always be a reflection of the human mind.

As dusk fell, a ripe moon rose up from behind the dunes on the far side of the lake and dripped light across the water. Our walk took us through a camping ground on the foreshore where everyone we passed seemed transfixed by the sight of this swollen orb. I thought of how Judith had walked here and seen the silhouettes of black swans crossing the moon, driven to the coast by drought. In their desolate cry, she had heard cry of the parched land. There were no swans on the lake this evening, but we had seen a few white egrets picking over the rocks near the sailing club beach. I still hoped that we might get lucky, as Judith did one evening when she saw, in a 'pool, jet-black and mirror-still', thirty egrets wading. As a girl, I had loved this poem 'Egrets' for its sense of momentousness and wonder. Now, more than ever, I felt I understood what she was trying to do. It is a poem that refrains from imposing any meaning or interpretation on what is witnessed, apart from communicating the poet's delight. Nothing eludes her because she is neither bent on capturing the birds as symbols nor the scene as an allegory. The poem simply celebrates the moment itself. As such, it foreshadows the tender detachment and careful observation of nature that would mark her final poems:

Once in a lifetime, lovely past believing,
your lucky eyes may light on such a pool.
As though for many years I had been waiting,
I watched in silence, till my heart was full
of clear dark water, and white trees unmoving,
and, whiter yet, those thirty egrets wading.

Although we didn't get lucky that evening, we saw one solitary bird that kept moving on as we approached, always threatening to launch into the air as if it feared we might want to catch it and pin it down in a poem.

The next morning we hired a small motor boat to take us across the lake and into the Upper Noosa River. Just to the north of Lake Cootharaba is the much smaller Lake Cooloola, which inspired 'At Cooloolah', one of Judith's most influential poems. The poem became a kind of anthem for the early conservation movement and was powerfully deployed in the campaign that stopped sand-mining in this vulnerable region of wildflower heaths, giant dunes, rainforests and freshwater lakes. The campaign, led by Kathleen McArthur and the Caloundra branch of the Wildlife Preservation Society of Queensland, showed what grass-roots activism could achieve. Joh Bjelke-Petersen, the most reactionary premier the country has ever known, had supported the mining but was forced to back down in the face of public opposition. In 1970, for the first time in Australian history, a government refused a mining venture in favour of a National Park.

If there are moments in history which mark a turning point in human values—the kind of shift in consciousness that shapes the lives of future generations—then Cooloola was one of them. After the Cooloola victory came the Great Barrier Reef and Fraser Island wins, all local indicators of a worldwide transformation in human understanding of our interdependent relationship with nature and this fragile planet.

The wind had dropped since the previous day and the dimpled brown water of the lake had a steely-blue tinge under a patchwork sky. The hire-boat man told us the lakes were not lakes at all but river flats—and shallow ones at that; we would easily stall if we didn't keep a watch on the depth. As we waded into the water, we could just make out the dusty green scrub-covered dunes on the far side of the lake, and a large, yellow sandy patch which marked the beginning of the Cooloola sandmass—the largest continuous series of sand dunes in the world. When navigating this coast, Captain Cook had used this sand blow as a marker. For the Aborigines of the region—the Dulingbara—it also held great significance as a lookout, a vantage point from which to survey the surrounding terrain.

Judith first saw this sand patch from the top of Mount Tinbeerwah in 1953. Inspired to investigate further, she took a boat across Lake Cootharaba 'so horizontal blue' to the Upper Noosa river. It thrilled her the way the river suddenly appeared out of nowhere, like a hidden entrance into another dimension as the boat went under an overhanging tree. The river, she reported back to her friends, was 'clear black like a mirror and covered with black swans and black ducks and bordered with huge tufts of ferns and flowers with overhanging trees reflected exactly in detail; and for miles and miles are queer deserted waterways and lakes, all different.'

We had been told to aim for the sand patch and keep between the channel markers. As yet, we could not see where the river began. We moved out into the middle of the lake and I began to register its size. Shattered sunlight danced in every direction. It seemed remarkable that this immense body of water was so close to Noosa yet remained so little known. Although Anna was a Queenslander and had been visiting Noosa for almost four decades, she had never been here and knew nothing about it. We had been let in on a special secret, a secret I was not sure I wanted to share. If mining had gone ahead, what would we have seen? Possibly, towards the north, a vast sand blow out of control. (Devastating dune instability had been the legacy of sand mining elsewhere.) There was enough sand in the Cooloola dunes to create a desert all the way to Gympie, forty kilometres inland.

As we approached the far end of the lake, the entrance to the Upper Noosa was still obscured. It wasn't until we navigated our way through the narrow channel between the land and Kinaba Island that we passed into the hidden opening and found ourselves at the secluded mouth of the river. The water, coloured by tannins from decayed vegetation, took on an ebony sheen and only then did I begin to understand Judith's obsession with the reflections this watery world threw back. Layers of transparent colour floated in the darkness—the pearly clouds, the blue sky, the pale bark of towering eucalypts and the green of overhanging branches. The riverbank—thick with reed-like sedges, paperbacks, native cotton trees studded with yellow flowers, giant mangroves, ferns and vines—glided by in an impenetrable wall that went deep down, in wavering replica, into the water beneath us.

We knew from the map that Lake Cooloola lay a few kilometres up river on the other side of that rainforest wall. When Judith went to Lake Cooloola with Kathleen, there had been a path from the river through the forest and the low-lying land beyond. The boatman had told us that the walking track to the lake had been left to grow over because it had become too swampy. Now, the lake can only be seen from a distance by walkers climbing the sand patch. The sight of this remote, pristine lake crystallised in Judith's mind why European-Australians felt so alienated from their native environment. Watching a blue crane fishing in the lake's shallows, it struck her suddenly that she could never share this bird's relationship with the land, its unconscious sense of belonging. The crane was 'the certain heir of the lake' but she was forever the outsider, 'a stranger, come of a conquering people'.

As we chugged very slowly up river, I tried to find gaps in the trees between us and the lake, tantalised by the thought of Lake Cooloola being so close yet out of reach. 'White shores of sand, plumed reed and paperbark, / clear heavenly levels frequented by crane and swan.' I told myself it was enough to know the lake was there, and that it had been saved. It would remain pristine, replenished by aquifers below the dunes and unsullied by human contact. For now, Lake Cooloola was a place that only poetry could take you to, like the western side of Mount Tamborine in Judith's poem 'Lyrebirds'. She chose not to go to there, to lyrebird country, she said, because 'Some things ought to be left secret, alone; / some things . . . / ought to inhabit nowhere but the reverence of the heart.'

But if I were to follow this logic, then why was I on this journey at all? The lyrebird is a symbol of 'the few, the shy, the fabulous, / the dying poets' and the poem is a warning against invading the poet's territory; just as Judith had tried, for most of her life, to keep biographers at bay. Hadn't I come to Boreen Point and Mount Tamborine hoping for echoes of the 'master practising [her] art'? The difference, I liked to think, was that my search was not for the poet but for the wellsprings of her art and activism in the landscapes she loved. The poetry had grown out of these landscapes, just as the plants in her garden had grown out of the red Mount Tamborine soil. Knowledge of these places may not be imperative to understanding her work, but I knew beyond doubt that my appreciation of her poetry was all the richer for having been here. To read her poems in light of this experience was like observing once-captive animals now released into their native habitat. They took on a whole new life when seen in the context from which they had sprung.

My rationalisation that Lake Cooloola was best left as a secret, a place inhabited only in the imagination, made me uneasy for another reason. By thinking of it in this idealised way, I avoided the human story which cast such a dark shadow over what Judith saw there. She had never been interested in wilderness for wilderness's sake. 'At Cooloolah' is explicitly about our relationship with the landscape and, more specifically, the relationship between blacks and whites. The poet feels 'unloved by all my eyes delight in' because of what her ancestors did to the land and the indigenous people. Judith was researching *The Generations of Men* at this time and was painfully conscious of her family's complicity in this process of dispossession. Hence, Cooloola felt like a place haunted by invisible presences that seemed to flicker at the edges of her vision. She remembered her grandfather Albert's story about coming across a solitary black warrior who vanished before his eyes. The 'dark-skinned people who once named Cooloola' might too have vanished, but they knew that 'earth is spirit' and that the land cannot be possessed. In trying to possess it, she concluded, we find ourselves in turn possessed by 'arrogant guilt', a guilt that reverberates down through the generations and touches us all.

In search of somewhere to have lunch, we moored at a small jetty not far from Kinaba Island and followed a path through the paper-bark forest and high native grasses. Suddenly, it opened out at a dreamy billabong dotted with native waterlilies whose pale pink flowers stood upright on long stems. The still brown pool was full of reflections—mostly shades of green and scraps of white cloud. I automatically thought of Monet's paintings, then stopped myself. Why couldn't I see the scene for what it was? Judith was constantly grappling with this dilemma: how to see and appreciate our natural environment on its own terms rather than through the filter of a European aesthetic. Two generations later, I still carried this baggage; still thought of Monet when I saw waterlilies. But the comparison jarred. More and more often, now, I saw things through Judith's eyes and through the prism of *her* art.

We were heading back down the river when we passed a large bleached trunk that had fallen into the water and was partially submerged. The way it curved and dipped under the water and reappeared again made me think of the Big Snake that was said to inhabit the lake. The story of Big Snake which 'had something to do with the rainbow' was told to Judith by some Aboriginal children who lived at Boreen Point in a fibro hut on the lakeside. She wrote about them in her short story 'At the Point' and in a slightly different, unpublished version which can be found in her papers called 'For Christine'. In both accounts, the Aboriginal family are treated as outcasts by the local community, but are befriended by Judith, Meredith and Jack. The father has come from a reservation, the mother is said to be an islander. In every way, they are made to feel that they do not belong. The four children may have no tribal connection with the area, but they bring to it what remains of their cultural inheritance: the lake is sacred to them because it is the home of Big Snake.

The story of Big Snake isn't mentioned in the published short story but is central to the version Judith wrote as a letter to the oldest girl, Christine, who had been Meredith's friend. Both versions end in tragedy: the father, Sam, goes on a drunken-bender and disappears for a few weeks. When he returns, his wife, Rosa, has taken up with a local fisherman, and he kills her in a fit of rage. Afterwards, the two

youngest are sent to a children's home, and Christine and the oldest
boy are sent to live with their grandfather on the notorious 'tropical
gulag' of Palm Island. Recollecting it all, Judith writes: 'Most of all I
remember you, Christine, . . . telling us the breathless story of the
Big Snake who made everything and then went to bed in the lake.'
As she knew when she wrote 'At Cooloolah', the beauty of these
lakes could not be divorced from their history and from the human
tragedy that lay so close to the surface.

Tragedy, it must have seemed to Judith, was never far from the
surface once you developed an eye for it. As we returned across the
lake, we passed a headland called Elanda Point, once known as Mill
Point after the sawmill which operated there from the 1860s to the
early 1890s. In its heyday, it was the biggest sawmill in Australia.
The company town that grew up around the mill was now an
archaeological site. Amongst the few remains—pylons from old jetties,
part of the original tramway, a brick chimney from a farmhouse—I
knew there was also a cemetery where four men, killed when a
boiler exploded at the mill in 1873, were buried. It was this event
that inspired Judith's poem 'The Graves At Mill Point'.

Back on shore, the boatman pointed us in the direction of an
overgrown path across open grassland that was supposed to lead to
the cemetery. After much tramping around, we eventually found a
triangular-shaped commemorative stone that had been erected 'in
memory of the European settlers buried at Mill Point Cemetery'.
Somewhere amidst the trees and high grass were the actual graves,
although most of the headstones were gone. Judith must have
wandered here amongst the bloodwood trees and heard the wind
through their branches, for it is this distinctive sound that she gives
voice to in her poem.

Much as she lamented the loss of the native trees that were felled
for the mill, she resisted the temptation to turn the explosion into
a morality tale about the consequences of recklessly exploiting the

land. Instead, she wrote an elegy in the form of a dialogue between one of the dead men and the wind through the bloodwood tree that grows over his grave. Like so many of her poems, it is haunted by voices from the past, and by the way time makes all that is solid melt into air. In Judith's version, the town dies with the men, and what remains becomes akin to the remnants of a bygone civilisation. For the dead men, the mourners and the town, this tragedy marks 'the end of the world'. Time washes away the words on the gravestones and all memory of the men is forgotten. Yet what the poem leaves us with is not a bleak sense of vanished lives, but of the intimate bond between the dead men and the natural world, suggested by the very name of the bloodwood tree which grows out of their bones and still 'flowers for their sake'.

That evening I went for a last walk by the lake. The place was deserted. Everyone must have been inside having dinner. There was no one at the beach, no boats on the water. No one wandering the shore. Even the birds seemed to have gone elsewhere. I had spent the day contemplating the ghosts that still lingered in the landscape. Now, I couldn't help thinking about what Boreen Point came to mean for Judith after Jack died.

Almost a year after his death in 1966, she told her close friend Barbara Blackman that she wasn't sure if she could bear coming back here. She began talking about selling the house two years later, but held on to it until 1973. Her final visit inspired 'Lake in Spring', a deeply personal echo of her earlier poem 'The Lake'. In it, she recalls walking by the lake with Jack and how their 'living looks met eye to eye' in its reflection. When she returns after his death, in 'another spring, another year', she bends to look into the water but 'the face that lay beside / my own, no longer answers there'. To read the poem is to understand why Boreen Point became, like Cooloola, a haunted place for Judith. Her world had changed utterly, yet the lake remained locked in an eternal present. It reflected back 'whatever comes, whatever goes / on path or hill', while being unable to hold any trace of the past or of the man she loved. Looking at her reflection, she was confronted not only by Jack's absence, but by the frightening erasure of memory the lake represented: the memory of all they had shared:

> A ripple goes across the glass.
> The faces break and blur and pass
> as love and time are blurred together.

THIRTEEN

Landscape of Grief

Two months before Jack's death in 1966, Judith and Jack went on a final journey together. Jack had recently finished *The Structure of Modern Thought*, the culmination of fifteen years' work on the philosophical underpinnings of the 'crisis of thought and feeling' afflicting the modern world. Judith asked Jack where he would like to go for a holiday. Jack decided on St George, 'an obscure hamlet', as Judith describes it, in south-west Queensland where he had taken a job droving cattle to Victoria in 1915, before joining the Light Horse. It was his way of revisiting 'his last year of innocence' before the horrors of war.

Jack was clearly unwell and had been for some time. His health had been particularly fragile since 1958 when he had suffered a heart attack. He was now 75. Judith's account of this final journey in an autobiographical fragment written in the months before her own death is her most heart-wrenching piece of prose. During the trip, Jack ate little and, even more distressing given what a great talker he was, he said little. Judith's mounting anxiety is evident from her descriptions of the landscape they travel through. As they crossed the Dividing Range, the bush gave way to cleared farmland. They stayed overnight at a pub but had to sleep in hard, single beds which made it impossible for them to hold each other. 'We had been for years without sexual contact but I liked to think that, even so, to be close was comforting to him as it was to me, and I lay awake thinking of the more than twenty years of warmth and partnership.'

The next day they drove through 'cruelly cleared country and bare plains of ploughed land'. So changed was it fifty years after that Jack did not recognise it. This wholesale clearing of vast tracts of Brigalow country, devastating soil and wildlife, would inspire Judith's most scathing poem, 'Australia 1970':

> Suffer, wild country, like the ironwood
> that gaps the dozer-blade.
> I see your living soil ebb with the tree
> to naked poverty.

She wrote this howl of rage, this furious curse on all our houses, when on an Adult Education tour through Queensland's Brigalow Belt in 1970. But the poem's mood of intense despair—'we are ruined by the thing we kill'—probably had its origins in her first experience of this country on this sad, final journey with Jack.

As the trip progressed, Jack fell silent. Judith captured their mutual misery through the bleakness of the landscape. They arrived at St George to find 'a bitterly eroded, riverside townlet' with weatherbeaten houses, few trees and 'gardens baked by all those passing days of sun and wind'. But the return journey to 'our gentler country' brought little comfort. When they got back to Mount Tamborine, Jack was diagnosed with inoperable stomach cancer.

A few months after his death, Judith referred to this final trip in a letter to her good friend, the poet Jack Blight. Unable to speak of the most distressing aspects of the journey, she wrote jauntily of 'the beautiful weather' and how 'we thoroughly enjoyed ourselves, driving off on to side roads, finding new kinds of bush flowers and drinking enormous beers in the pubs en route. Not as much fun as camping out—but we were a bit past that stage and stayed in motels instead.' Desperate to make the best of a deeply painful memory, she concluded: 'It was a very good finale to all our camping holidays together.'

Judith's journey through the landscape of grief had just begun, and would continue for many years. She would give away little of her feelings in her letters, but would chart the contours of this grim terrain in her dreams and poems.

Six weeks after Jack died, Judith had a dream in which she found herself on yet another journey: she, Meredith and a friend set out to walk around Cape Horn (presumably South America). The dream took her through many different landscapes including a polluted creek, reminiscent of that behind the hospital where Jack died. Judith knew that the journey would be a long one but found comfort in the knowledge that others had done it before them. She also knew that she and Meredith would have to take separate paths. Eventually, she found herself on a beach which reminded her of one she visited with Jack the year before when they had been so happy. The dream ended with a voice telling her to 'Linger by this pool. Here your structural problems will be solved.'

Judith understood this to mean that she shouldn't leave Tamborine yet. She and Meredith had moved to a flat in Brisbane while Meredith completed her final year at school. She still felt deeply connected with the mountain, however, and looked forward to returning there on weekends. 'It's so good getting back there, with the garden to dig in,' she wrote to a friend. Being at Tamborine made her feel like 'a real person again'. Later in that year, after a trip to Canada for a literary festival, she told Barbara Blackman that she physically ached for Tamborine—another way of saying how much she ached for Jack. Her love for him would always be inseparable from the landscape where they had felt so blessed.

> Here still, the mountain that we climbed
> when hand in hand my love and I
> first looked through one another's eyes
> and found the world that does not die.

Much as she longed for the mountain, each return journey was a painful reminder of Jack's absence. Even the landscape felt dramatically changed. The world that she had shared with Jack had been full of brilliant flowers, aromatic plants and stars that 'circled round us where we lay'. Now, it was as if she were climbing the mountain with her bare hands, facing 'steep unyielding rock, / . . . struggling the upward path again, / this time alone.' Her poetry about this grief-stricken period shows her withdrawing into a place beyond the reach of the outside world. She remains vaguely aware of life going on around her but it feels removed, mechanical and uncaring. At her most bleak, she sees herself as Eurydice in hell. The contours of the mountain are there—two lovers walking hand in hand along a path. But then the path suddenly collapses, as if in a landslide, and traps her beneath the earth in a nightmare world of clay corridors and blind passages. A recurring feature of this psychic landscape is its deathly silence: the silence she fears she is condemned to now that Jack, who had so inspired her, is gone. In a letter to a fellow poet, she wrote forlornly of her hope that she might eventually get another book written. At present, though, she was 'stuck at the bottom of a page as though it were a cliff edge.'

Eight months after Jack's death, Judith had a dream that Meredith came to her during the night to tell her that 'something is wrong with Dad'. She found him in Meredith's room, invisible except for his vestigial blue pyjamas, trying to get under one of the beds. Once her arms were around him, Judith recognised his shape and was filled with great joy. She helped him lie down on Meredith's bed and reassured him that he was only ill, that everything was all right; he was back with them. When she woke up, it was midnight and she could still feel his shape, warm and real and strong as before, in her arms.

When I returned to Mount Tamborine a second time, I drove up the old road. The first time, on the 'do-it-yourself road', I had seen the developed side of the mountain—the housing estates, the cleared rural land, the Gold Coast in the distance—before I saw any forest. And then, once on the mountain, I had been primed to see how little remained of the original vegetation—the National Parks seemed mere scraps of land, sad fragments or remnants of the once great rainforest that had been here. But this time, I saw things differently. After the rural lowlands came the thick sclerophyll forests which slowly gave way higher up to the damp world of the rainforest, the darkness intensified by the brightness of the day. I felt I was seeing the mountain as Judith and Jack had known it, and was reminded of what Meredith told me about her experience of coming back here. How she saw only what she knew from childhood and was able to ignore what had changed. She was pleasantly surprised by how much remained as she remembered it, even down to the particular roots of trees on the forest paths.

I could see the wisdom in this way of viewing things. Having grown up on the mountain, Meredith accepted it—as all children do—for what it was without being troubled by what had once been. But, by the time Judith came here, she was acutely attuned to the wounds in any landscape. Meredith remembers that often on their travels Judith would point out the damage that had been done to the environment, particularly soil erosion which had been a major problem at Wallamumbi. While this was not an easy or comfortable way to live— as most activists know too well—without this heightened sensitivity to what was gone, she would not have done or foreseen all that she did.

Much as I was glad to see the mountain in a positive light, I was still conscious of the changes. What saddened me the most was very small in the scale of things—the disappearance of the flame-tree Jack had planted near the front gate, not long after they moved to 'Calanthe'—yet of enormous personal significance for Judith because it was a living symbol of their love. I had searched long and hard for this tree the day Anna and I visited Calanthe. But neither of us knew what such a plant looked like when it wasn't in flower. I had a vague sense of where it should be and plucked leaves from trees I thought might be it. Later that day, I took the leaves to a nursery up the road but was told that none belonged to the flame-tree. In a month's time, the flame-trees would drop their leaves and burst into a teeming, dazzling mass of tiny scarlet bells, but not yet. A week after I returned home from that first trip, Anna told me that the flame-trees in Brisbane had started to bloom.

Judith devoted three poems to this tree and referred to it in a number of others. Flame-trees do grow wild on the mountain but, even before she moved here, she had fallen in love with the ones she had seen in Brisbane. Her first flame-tree poem was inspired by the sight of one growing out of a quarry like a 'fountain of hot joy'. A quarry is a classic image of wounded landscape, which made the sight of it growing from this 'wrecked skull' all the more exhilarating. With its distinct echoes of Christian resurrection, the poem reminded me of the more joyful hymns I had sung as a child at church:

> Out of the torn earth's mouth
> comes the old cry of praise.
> Still is the song made flesh
> though the singer dies—

The rapture the poet experiences is not that of being filled with the spirit of Christ, but with the spirit of earthly desire, the sense of being born again through love—which was exactly what Judith had experienced with Jack.

Long before their own flame-tree bloomed, Judith would feast her eyes on the tree that grew on the hill above the creek behind Calanthe. She described it to Kathleen McArthur as being 'one huge blaze'. For her part, Kathleen would remember the year they met as one of 'great blossoming of the mountain's flame trees'. This particular tree was 'the most inspiring of all flame-trees' she had seen.

Bookshop shelves groan with self-help guides offering advice on how to be happy, how to get the most out of life, how to find our 'true' selves, but Judith found the answers to these questions in the flame-tree she could see from her back steps. By dropping its leaves before it blooms, the tree gives its entire being over to the act of flowering and then, having blossomed, carelessly scatters its flowers with generous abandon. The answer that came to her 'this sudden season' was to live and love in the same way: passionately, without reserve, always giving oneself fully to the moment and to others. One finds oneself by losing oneself in the act of love. The poem concludes with the gratitude 'of lovers who share one mind', a phrase she would echo in a later poem addressed to Jack: 'the equal heart and mind' who answers her love 'in kind'.

Meredith remembers how much her parents looked forward to seeing their own flame-tree bloom, how year after year they would ask, 'Will the tree flower this summer?' The intense emotion they all invested in this tree makes Judith's final flame-tree poem particularly devastating. The tree eventually flowered after Jack's death, but brought none of the anticipated joy. Its final eruption into flower only reminded her of what she had lost, and what they had longed to share:

> Now, in its eighteenth spring,
> suddenly, wholly, ceremoniously
> it puts off every leaf and stands up nakedly,
> calling and gathering,
>
> every capacity in it, every power,
> drawing up from the very roots of being
> this pulse of total red that shocks my seeing
> into an agony of flower.

The first time I went to the Mount Tamborine cemetery I couldn't find Jack's grave. The cemetery is not big, but for some reason Jack's eluded me. I returned the next day with local historian, Paul Lyons, who took me straight to it. There is no slab and the granite headstone is a small one, which perhaps accounts for why I had overlooked it. It reads: 'Jack Philip McKinney, 1891–1966, Let the spirit of Truth dwell with me'. Below his inscription is Judith's, added later: 'Judith Wright McKinney, 1915–2000'. Underneath both is written: 'United in Truth'.

I stood on the grassy slope by the grave, looking out over the Witches Falls National Park that lies directly behind the cemetery. 'Not till those fiery ghosts are laid / shall we be one,' Judith had written during their early years on the mountain. Those fiery ghosts were the many complications in their relationship—Jack's marriage, her disapproving family, a child out of wedlock, their odd existence as a poet and philosopher in a conservative rural community. At that time, it felt to her as if all things conspired to stand between them.

Yet, as the poem acknowledges, this feeling of being outsiders, of living on the margins of 'respectable society', sharpened their ability to see the world for what it was. And now here, in this grave on the edge of the mountain, those ghosts had been laid for good.

Towards evening, I wandered a little further up the road to what Judith called 'Jack's seat'. It is a spot with a panoramic view over the western edge of the mountain, the foothills and checkered farmland below. After Jack's death, Charles and Barbara Blackman paid for a wooden seat with a plaque to be erected in his memory at the spot where Jack and Judith often went to watch the sun set. Judith told Barbara that one evening, when she was sitting there, she heard a butcher-bird 'whistling one of Jack's tunes'. Not long before she left the mountain for good, she was delighted to see a group of 'rather beautiful people sitting on Jack's seat, watching the sunset and kissing each other.'

The original seat has been replaced with a conventional park bench made of wooden slats, and a plaque dedicated to Judith has been added. Curiously, it does not mention that she was our greatest poet, but simply describes her as Jack's wife. I sat, shivering a little, as dusk fell and watched the low sun disappear behind a thick band of gun-metal cloud. A halo of light escaped from around its edges, just enough to bathe the landscape in a gentle glow. Much of the mountain has a shadowy, closed-in feel from the fringes of rainforest. But, here, everything opens out. Despite the noise of cars speeding past on the road behind me, I could see why Jack and Judith loved this spot. To look out over the foothills and into the distance was to be left with a sudden feeling of expansiveness and relief; a tantalising sense of being, if only for a moment, above the cares of the world.

Judith returned to live at Calanthe in 1968, after six months in Europe with Meredith. She had missed the mountain and was glad to be back in her own house and garden. Over the years, her house had come to feel like an extension of her body, her native habitat. Meditating on the time she had spent here, she recalled the eight-foot carpet-snake that used to winter in the ceiling and eat the rats, and the blossom-bat that, like a small fur umbrella, used to hang in her bedroom, and the mud-wasps that built cells in hollows under books. She recalled the three-day cyclone which made the house roll like a wooden ship, and the long heat-wave that made the weatherboards crack and shrink.

Sometimes, lost in thought or reading, she would raise her eyes and a shadow would suggest Jack in his old chair. And yet his absence was as real to her now as his presence had once been. Sometimes, she was able to think of his absence as a positive reminder of the 'secret place behind the world'; to feel his silence as part of an on-going dialogue. But most of the time, it was just silence—an unbridgeable gulf.

Judith still took great delight in her garden but, as the years passed, the two acres became increasingly difficult for her to manage on her own. 'The garden is so huge and wild with trees I am practically a jungle woman,' she wrote to Barbara. Yet she was reluctant to leave Calanthe because of all the memories it held— 'the best of my life has been lived here'. Even in the year before she moved south to Braidwood, in early 1976, she still felt a 'rush of come-homeness and the peace' whenever she returned from her travels to Mount Tamborine. 'So many places I can see Jack standing or sitting, that'll be hard to leave . . .' At the same time, she knew she was ready to go.

As her conservation work took her away more often and her relationship with Nugget Coombs began to develop in the early 1970s, her poems and dreams revealed a process of gradual detachment from Mount Tamborine and from Jack. In one poem that harks back to Boreen

Point, she writes of a 'half-dream' about an old boat tied up on the shore of a lake. In this semi-conscious state, the poet is aware of the mooring rope wearing away. By the end, she has accepted that it must eventually fray and, by implication, break. And yet the deep attachment she felt to Jack endured, even after Nugget became her lover.

Judith and Nugget had been together for seven years when she had a dream that finally 'released' her. She could see the earth from a great distance, as if from outer space—an image clearly inspired by the pictures transmitted during the moon missions in the 1960s. She had already written about these images of our 'tiny vulnerable planet', and how they marked the first time that humans had had the chance to see the planet as a whole, to see it as the astronauts had, as 'beautiful and frail and small, and above all as 'home''. In her dream, the earth looked like a precious stone and it wrung her heart to leave it, but it was diseased. She woke in tears, knowing that she had been 'detached from some bond, like having a sinew very gently parted. As though someone, a mother or father, pulled your hand gently away from holding one thing and transferred it to holding something else.'

Then she went back to sleep and dreamed again. She was lying in bed and could hear, on the other side of the wall, a child crying in the dark. She was afraid it was a demon 'Rakshasa'—the man-eating Hindu spirit mentioned in the book, *Descent of the Sun*, she was reading at the time. Although it was 'one of the dead', she was filled with love and longing for it. She called out and heard it reply. She kept calling and the child-demon slowly approached and stood by her bed in the darkness. Terrified yet entranced, she crooned and enticed it into her bed. Then she realised it was Jack and was filled with great joy, and knew that she had been set free.

Jack had been her 'earth' but it was time to let go of him. Over a decade had passed since his death, and she had found a new love and a new plot of earth on which to live. As she prepared to leave her garden at Tamborine—cutting back fleshy stems and smelling the gardenias—she thought of the stony ridge far to the south that lay 'waiting for me to know it'. She thought of the cold wind off the snowy mountains, and the small 'white-etched trees' and of the morning frosts there. She was in the autumn of her life now, and the summery, subtropical world of Tamborine with all its extravagant growth was no longer in keeping with who she was.

> I'm tired now, summers,
> of cutting you back to size.
> Where I'm going you will be more succinct;
> just time for a hurried embroidery
> of bed, leaf, flower, seed
> before the snow-winds snip you
> to a root's endurance.

It was hot the day I drove down the mountain. Once again, I took the old, windy road through tunnels of shade and sudden shafts of sunlight. Not long after the rainforest gave way to dry eucalypt forest, I turned off to Cedar Creek Falls. As soon as I was out of the car, I heard the sound of water falling and saw a group of teenagers heading across the carpark towards me, their hair dripping and faces glowing. A short walk along a well-established path led to the white gush of the falls, which plunged into a pool far below, before tumbling down an even more precipitous drop into a larger pool, and then continuing its course down the mountain. Everywhere there were signs warning of the dangers of the slippery rocks and ledges. Anyone who wanted to get to the rockpools was instructed to take the path. All other methods of access were prohibited.

Not long before Judith left Mount Tamborine, she wrote a poem called 'At Cedar Creek'. She was more heavily involved than ever before with environmental campaigns and, increasingly, with indigenous issues. Her years of activism and her relationship with Nugget, who had become one of Prime Minister Whitlam's advisers, had allowed her to observe the workings of power from close range. She was still writing poetry, but her exposure to the language and mentality of politics, bureaucracy and the media, had left her questioning her past conviction that poetry could make things happen; that it could change people's consciousness for the better. Under the influence of Jung, she had written poetry that mapped our psychic landscape in the hope that it would help us better understand our interdependent relationship with the real landscape. But, now, she wasn't so sure.

As I stood looking out over the falls, I thought about how far Judith had, by this time, grown away from the world of Tamborine and all it had once represented to her. In 'At Cedar Creek', she abandons her garden—which represents the vision she and Jack once shared— and heads for the waterfalls here at Cedar Creek National Park. Her lobbying and activism have left her head reeling with political slogans and headlines. Everything she contemplates—including poetry—feels polluted by this reductive way of thinking, just as nature has been polluted. 'How,' she asks, 'shall I remember the formula for poetry?' She even finds herself satirising the preoccupations she once held dear—mythology, primitive cultures and psychoanalytic thought. She used to believe that the wisdom of these disciplines, distilled into poetry, could help foster a higher level of ecological awareness and emotional intelligence that would revolutionise our relationship with the natural world. Now, all she can see are the contradictions, the flaws in any form of reasoning which applies knowledge in a purely utilitarian way, or regards human experience as an equation to be solved. Our over-analytical minds have led us to become reductive and schematic, cutting us off from the pulse of life. As she writes in another poem, 'Whatever Being is . . . / it dies as we pursue it past the word. / We have not asked the meaning, but the use.'

Heading back towards the carpark, I watched some more teenagers—this time, clutching beer bottles—approaching down the path. Before our paths crossed, they ducked under the railing. With the confidence of those who had done it many times before, they made their way down the foot-worn and risky-looking track next to the waterfall. Soon they were diving into the pools below. The signs might as well not have been there. It must have struck Judith, at some point, that her poems had become akin to these ineffectual signs warning people of the dangers of going beyond the barriers. Signs that were blithely ignored.

Judith had lost her faith in the power of poetry to change the world, and the muse was beginning to desert her. She would produce only one more collection before she stopped writing verse for good. It was clear to her now that the 'mythopoetic connection to the landscape' she had once hoped to foster could not save the planet. Her dream in which she saw the earth from a great distance and felt that she had been detached from some bond was not just about Jack; it also marked her disengagement from poetry and her decision to devote herself almost entirely to activism. Grass-roots environmental work—campaigning to save the Great Barrier Reef, Cooloola and Fraser Island and, later, her involvement in the political process in Canberra—had shown what could be achieved through direct action. From now on, this would be where most of her creative energy would go.

Losing the 'formula' for poetry was not, then, a reason to despair. When she had woken from that dream, these words had stayed with her: *To lose one's grasp is to gain a new grasp of something.* 'Losing the first was grief,' she wrote the next morning in her diary, 'but the new thing was much more important.'

Canberra & Mongarlowe

FOURTEEN

Opera City

It was early autumn—a year since I had begun this journey—and
Canberra's many poplars were beginning to turn gold. Each day, I
would walk from my friends' flat in Lyneham (just north of the centre),
through the city centre itself, and then across the Commonwealth
Avenue Bridge to where the National Library sat like a giant marble
treasure box on the shores of Lake Burley Griffin. The walk was a long
one and I was always struck by how few pedestrians there were, apart
from in the city centre. I was not sure I would ever feel comfortable
with the monumental scale of the city; it seemed to discourage
intimacy. As I walked the wide, empty streets and scurried ant-like
across the massive roundabouts, glimpsing the hump of Parliament
House in the distance, I could understand why Judith saw the city
as a 'fantas[y] of power', a kind of mirage.

In the poem 'Brief Notes on Canberra' she imagines a time
before the city was built: the city's architect Walter Burley Griffin
surveys 'The tawny basin in the ring of hills' and sees an *empty space*
waiting to be filled by his 'rhetorical opera-city', with 'great circles'

and 'radials'. But nature was never empty for Judith. Her awareness of what had been here before, heightened by the ever-looming hills and open spaces, only reinforced her sense of the city's uncanniness, its artificiality.

From the window of the flat where she stayed at University House, she looked out on a huge eucalypt much older than the city itself. It was sights such as this that made Canberra livable for her. Not surprisingly, the European trees struck her as forlornly out of place, lining the roads like an official welcome, always on guard. When considered as an ecosystem, Canberra was 'impossible'. Deliberately adopting the sterile language of a bureaucratic report, she declared that as a monoculture it ought to be unstable: 'No balance between input and output.' There were too many predators, too few producers and too few refuges for prey. That the city continued to exist, she wryly concluded, was 'an ecological miracle'.

While she didn't feel any great attachment to the city itself, she *was* deeply attached to one particular Canberra resident, Herbert Cole 'Nugget' Coombs, who lived at the Australian National University's residence, University House. Each day, after immersing myself in their newly released letters in the Manuscripts Reading Room at the National Library of Australia, I would emerge with a mounting respect for the way they conducted themselves in this relationship; the way they forged their own private realm while remaining answerable to the public world in which they were both so active. It astounded me that their desire for privacy, even after death, had been observed for so long. Until the release of these letters in 2009, the relationship had been one of the best kept open secrets in Australian literary history.

Judith first met Nugget in the 1960s when he was then chairman of the Council for the Arts. He asked her to become a member and, although she couldn't take up his invitation, they stayed in touch, exchanging views on the arts, Aboriginal issues and the environment. Nugget was a prominent and extraordinarily influential bureaucrat, about whom Judith had known for decades, just as he had known of her. She first became aware of him as the economist who played a leading role in planning the rationing system during the war. He became a household name as Director-General of Post-War Reconstruction and, when he was made Governor of the Reserve Bank in 1949, his signature on banknotes suggested to her a man of even-handedness and balance. This impression was confirmed when he retained his role as adviser to seven Labor and Liberal federal governments, proving the wisdom of his non-partisan advice. As his concern about the impact of economics and industry on the environment began to grow, along with his advocacy for the arts and his commitment to Aboriginal land rights, their passions began to converge.

After Judith's death, Meredith found a note Nugget had written to Judith. It was a fragment of a conversation, scribbled down because Judith could no longer hear. In it, Nugget reminded her of their first night together after a meeting they'd both attended. In 1972, Judith introduced Nugget to her daughter as the new love in her life. Judith was fifty-seven, Nugget was sixty-six. Ten years before, she had written a poem called 'Prayer', a plea to the muse not to desert her as she ages. Its opening line, however, addresses a more fundamental fear: 'Let love not fall from me though I must grow old.' In this respect, her prayer was answered.

By the time their relationship began, they were both well-known public figures—the distinguished yet down-to-earth statesman and the famous poet-cum-activist. As *éminences grises*, both had reputations to live up to and responsibilities that often trumped their individual desires. The tension between the demands of public life and private needs was something they would struggle with throughout their relationship. Nugget and his wife, Mary, were estranged, but his loyalty to her and to his children meant that he never contemplated a divorce. According to Meredith, Judith was even more determined than Nugget to keep the relationship secret because she still carried guilt about the pain she felt she'd caused Jack's family when they first met.

In her public writing, Judith spoke of Nugget as a valued and respected colleague. She was always careful to keep her tone detached and professional. Nugget, who was a less reserved person, did not feel quite so constrained. In his book *Aboriginal Autonomy*, published in 1994, he warmly acknowledged his fruitful thirty-year partnership with Judith. 'Indeed,' he wrote, 'it is difficult for me to identify much which was not, to a greater or lesser degree, the product of that partnership.'

Their letters make plain that their passion for Aboriginal rights and the environment was inseparable from their passion for each other. This is not to downplay the physical chemistry between them: Nugget was a charming man with a mischievous smile who was very appealing to women. Meredith remembers him as a 'darling person'. Judith's slightly gruff, patrician manner, which masked an intense emotional life and a generous spirit, held its own appeal. Nugget found her poetry very moving and his letters to her usually began: 'My lovely woman'. But both were too committed to social reform to be interested in a purely romantic liaison.

Mutual concern for the common good and for their private obligations would ensure that they maintained appearances until the end. It's a stance that, in a culture obsessed with celebrity and self-exposure, can seem heroically quaint. Not once did they attend an official function together as a couple or publicly declare their love. In April 1975, with her sixtieth birthday looming, Judith wrote to Nugget: 'Barbara Blackman wants to give me a birthday party and asks who I would want to ask. Well—but perhaps not. Only a couple of weeks, but it's a long time, my love.'

Over their twenty-five years together, they would write hundreds of letters to one another, sometimes at a rate of three a week. But the story of the relationship as told through the correspondence is inescapably dominated by Judith's voice, as only a fraction of Nugget's letters remain. I knew from having read many of Judith's other letters that it would be unwise to expect ardent lyricism or sensational revelations. The letter had never been a form of literary expression for her. It was a tool, a way of maintaining friendships, of intellectual exchange and of making things happen. As a correspondent her voice was very much like her spoken voice: matter-of-fact, practical, wry. All her pain and passion went into her verse. Although Judith's letters to Nugget bear little resemblance to a conventional love letter, there is no doubt that they document a profound and lasting bond.

The more I read of the letters, the more I became aware of how the need for secrecy, their work and, later, their health problems kept them apart—and how much they missed each other. There were times when I found myself wishing they would just ditch their commitments and wander off into the sunset together. They did vaguely entertain the idea, but this Hollywood fantasy was never a real option for them. I had to keep reminding myself that letters, by their nature, document periods of separation. Judith and Nugget also had much time together—time they savoured because they knew it was short.

When the relationship began in 1972, Judith was still living at Calanthe and commuting regularly to Canberra, Sydney and elsewhere to attend meetings, address rallies, go to protest marches and lobby politicians, while constantly writing papers, books, poetry, reports and letters. She was still heavily involved in the Wildlife Preservation Society of Queensland as its president, but campaigns like those to save the Great Barrier Reef and Fraser Island had now become national issues. She had also helped found the national Project to Stop the Concorde, opposing plans to establish a supersonic corridor across Australia that would subject Aboriginal people living in inland Australia to the aircraft's sonic boom, as well as threatening the ozone layer.

Whenever she was in Canberra, she would stay with Nugget in his flat at University House. The position they found themselves in was not unlike the position she and Jack had been in when they first met in Brisbane. They could not live together and, as yet, they did not have a shared landscape. What they did have, though—as did Judith and Jack—and what sustained them in these early days, was a common intellectual terrain and a passion for social reform. This shared landscape took its contours, as had Judith and Jack's, from the idealism of the immediate post-war period. But, now, it was informed by the new language of conservation and Aboriginal land rights. As I sat in the National Library with the boxes of letters in front of me, I felt like an early explorer finally granted entry to an unmapped landscape: the place where their minds met.

In the 1960s, the emergence of ecology as a discipline had given conservationists a scientific grounding for their arguments about the interconnectedness of all life on earth and the importance of balance between the natural and man-made world. Ecology as a concept has its roots in the eighteenth century when it was known as 'the economy of nature'. This crucial nexus of ecosystems and economies was a subject that would preoccupy Judith and Nugget's earliest exchanges. Although most economists at this time paid little heed to the environmental costs of modern consumer society, Nugget was just beginning to turn his attention to the issue.

In her own writing, Judith had long been voicing alarm about the way economic thinking flew in the face of environmental realities. To read her many forceful essays from the 1960s onward is to be struck—yet again—by how prescient she was and how slow we have been to catch on. Current debates about global warming still lag behind her recognition that the problem 'entails a whole new philosophy of living, a whole new social and legal dispensation, a new kind of education and new kind of government' including a new form of economics 'based firmly on the biosphere itself and its own support systems.'

As well as discussing her views with him, Judith would send Nugget recent articles on ecology to help him clarify his own arguments. Their message, however, was not one that politicians and the business world were ready to hear. After his death, Judith reflected that 'climate change, pollution of land and sea, ozone loss have become obvious since that time and cannot be disputed any longer. But he suffered a good deal from his first-footing in such subjects.' She had long known that the outspoken conservationist was invariably seen as 'a Cassandra prophesying woe—he may be right but he will not be popular.'

Just as Judith was influential in deepening Nugget's understanding of environmental issues, Nugget's commitment to Aboriginal autonomy and land rights deepened and radicalised her understanding of Indigenous affairs. As Chair of the Council for Aboriginal Affairs in the late 1960s and early 1970s, he saw the destructive effect of assimilation policy and became a believer in the importance of allowing Aborigines to determine their own future. Throughout his relationship with Judith, this was his overriding obsession, and it increasingly became Judith's also. What began as an intuitive understanding of the tragedy that haunted the New England landscape and later deepened into an emotional bond through her friendship with the Aboriginal poet, Kath Walker (Oodgeroo Nounuccal), now found intellectual substance and rigour through her conversations and travels with Nugget.

Appropriately, for a couple dedicated to social reform, their love affair began in the year the Whitlam government came to power. But, as heady a time as it was, their new responsibilities immediately put pressure on the relationship. The formality of Judith's early letters to Nugget suggests that she was wary, at first, of putting her feelings to paper, and that she suspected his position as Whitlam's special adviser and head of the new arts body, the Australia Council would consume much of his time. Within a year, her tone had relaxed. While she fretted that Nugget was being asked to do too much, too quickly, she was grateful for the government's responsiveness on environmental issues, particularly the declaration of the Great Barrier Reef and Fraser Island as National Parks. In 1974, she was appointed to the Inquiry into the National Estate, which advised on the protection of cultural and natural heritage—everything from historic buildings to National Parks. This demanded much travel around the country, after which she had the task of editing a massive report.

As exhilarating as this period was, she found life in Canberra unsettling. 'Everything here is immediately related to political endgames and seen in terms of advantage for one side or the other; a city that has so few pensioners, people over 60, and ordinary workin' types and is so nicely cushioned against most things isn't part of the real world to me.' She was a territorial animal, as she remarked to a friend, and Canberra wasn't her territory. She had never been fond of cities. Nothing was more real to her than the natural world and she was beginning to hanker for it.

When Nugget heard that land at the Half Moon Wildlife District, not far from the town of Braidwood, one hundred kilometres east of Canberra, was up for sale, he told Judith and they went to look at it. She immediately fell in love with this 'long slope that goes down to a still wild and unpolluted river'. The landscape here on the south-east edge of the southern tableland reminded her of the 'lean, hungry country' of New England, where she grew up. As she didn't have quite enough money to buy it, Nugget helped out and also put money towards the building of the house.

'The land's so lovely I can't believe I've really got it,' Judith told friends. 'The ridges are all ironstone quartz conglomerate rocks with all manner of wild-flowers.' Her excitement also had much to do with the fact that she and Nugget would now have a place of their own, a private sanctuary where their love could find its fullest expression. While the fall of the Whitlam government in 1975 left them both disillusioned, it also marked the beginning of a new and thrilling phase in their lives.

FIFTEEN

The World's Last Edge

It was late afternoon when the bus pulled into the goldfields town of Braidwood with its wrought-iron verandas, heavy stone buildings and sleepy, country air. Meredith was waiting for me at the stop. It wasn't hard to pick her. Although she has her father's fine features, she is unmistakably her mother's daughter when she smiles.

We drove down the main street past an old, colonial-style bank which was now a gallery and cafe called Studio Altenburg. She and Judith had lived there in 1976 while the house was being built at Edge, and while Meredith was completing her doctoral thesis at the Australian National University on a wandering Japanese Buddhist monk and poet, Saigyo. After finishing school, Meredith had studied Japanese at university, done further study in Kyoto and then begun teaching English at various universities there. After twenty years in Japan, she now lived on her own bush property not far from 'Edge' and translated Japanese literature into English for a living. She had called her hundred acres of eucalypt forest 'Yuen'—Japanese for garden of serenity—and in acknowledgment of the Yuin Aboriginal tribe who had lived there.

Once we were out of town, Meredith pointed to the rocky outcrops of granite pushing up through the open farmland. On the crest of one hill sat a row of large grey boulders, the configuration of which gave it the air of an ancient sacred site. In other places, clusters of smaller rocks huddled together like sheep. It was easy to see why this landscape had reminded Judith of New England. The weather, too, would have reinforced this sense of familiarity—frosts in winter, crisp dry air and parched summers. She must have felt in her bones that she had come full circle; that in a fundamental way, she had come home. And yet there was more to it than this. Part of Judith's attraction to Edge, as I would discover, was that it required her to surrender the last vestiges of her dream of returning to that 'lost garden' of childhood. In the end, she knew that being 'at home' in the landscape was quite different to recapturing the landscape of one's youth.

That night, I slept in the guest room of Meredith's exquisitely proportioned, rammed-earth house—the room in which Judith used to sleep whenever she came to stay. Judith would spend one week here every month when she became too frail to live alone at Edge and had moved back to the old bank in the township of Braidwood. The cow bell that Jack used to ring to call Judith in from the veggie garden at Calanthe now sat by the bed. On the wall near the door hung Charles Blackman's stark but moving portrait of Jack.

The next morning I was woken by a bird fluttering at the high small window opposite the bed, tapping a repeated tattoo on the glass, as if it had an urgent message to communicate. When I told Meredith about it, she said that just after Judith's death, one of these birds—a shrike thrush—started visiting this particular window, sitting on the sill and tapping at the glass. It was now tame and came to the door every morning to be fed. Judith had believed that birds were spirit carriers, Meredith added, leaving the implications hanging. I told her about the large lizard we saw near Council Rock at Wallamumbi and how we had joked about it being a visitation from her mother.

We sat near the bay window which overlooks a native garden of banksias, grevilleas and a small paved courtyard area with a Japanese-style pond. Before the garden was landscaped, Judith had noticed that water gathered in a slight depression and suggested to Meredith that it would make a good place for a pond. The positioning could not have been better. As we ate our breakfast, the morning sun reflecting off the water danced in bright patches on the high, cathedral ceiling of the living room. Once she'd become totally deaf, Judith took extra pleasure in what her eyes could feast on and loved to sit here and watch the play of light.

With the sun streaming through the window, Meredith told me about a dream she'd had the night before. She and Judith were in a house together that kept shifting location. Meredith tried to tell Judith what was happening but her mother didn't understand until she went outside and saw that the landscape had changed. They were so disorientated they had to go and ask the neighbours where they were. It turned out that the house was on wheels and moved of its own accord with the wind.

Like her mother, Meredith has a propensity for searing, visceral dreams. The day before, she had told me about a 'big dream' she'd once had about Judith. It was still playing on my mind because it raised such confronting questions about what people like me, who went looking for the woman behind the poems, expected to find. In Judith's later years, Meredith was conscious of her mother's life being transformed into legend. After Judith's death, media and public attention was intense, leaving Meredith with little room for her own private grief, for the fact that it was her *mother* who had died, not the famous poet and activist everyone else imagined they knew.

The dream, which Meredith had had long before the Two Fires Festival was established at Braidwood, was about a literary festival honouring Judith at Calanthe. Meredith was invited and, although she found the idea painful, she felt that she ought to be there as her mother's representative. The festival began in the study, the front room of the house, where Judith had worked. A number of people gave papers about Judith as a poet. Sitting in the front row of the audience, Meredith was aware that her reactions were being monitored; she smiled encouragingly because she felt it was expected of her. The next part of the proceedings took place in the room next to the study, Meredith's old bedroom, where she used to fall asleep to the sound of her mother's typewriter. Here, she found it harder to participate because this room had once been her private space. Someone got up and began to talk about objects that had once belonged to Judith— personal items, things Meredith remembered from around the house—and the speaker was getting it wrong. Meredith didn't want to contradict them in public but, on the other hand, she wanted to protect the truth. In a state of turmoil, she felt obliged to remain supportive even as her and her mother's past was being violated.

The *pièce de résistance* of the dream festival was a special display in Judith and Jack's old bedroom. Propped up against the wall was a life-size, wax dummy of Judith which was said to be wearing her clothes. Meredith remembered the old blouse from the fifties, but knew the skirt had been made from the curtain that had hung between Meredith's bedroom and the main bedroom. This was disturbing enough in itself. Then the guide lifted one of the dummy's inert arms and dropped it, remarking that they hadn't got the exhibit quite right yet. Meredith watched in horror: the dummy was not a waxwork but her mother's corpse. At this point, she rushed out of the room in tears.

'When I woke up, I thought, that's how it feels—that sense of everybody wanting a bit of her, the whole myth-making thing.'

There wasn't a lot I could say in reply. In self-defence, I said I hoped that whatever I wrote would not feel like a violation to her, and that my main interest was in how the landscape had shaped Judith's vision as a writer and an activist. But, of course, much as I disliked the grosser invasions of biography, I *had* intruded on her private life and there was no getting away from that.

A five-minute drive along the road through the hamlet of Mongarlowe brought us to the Half Moon Wildlife District, three hundred and eighty hectares of land on a high ridge that slopes down towards the Mongarlowe River. In the distance to the east loomed the 'black calligraphy' of the Budawung Ranges. When I had arrived at Braidwood the previous day, I had no memory of having been there before. But now the sight of Edge and the A-frame house which Judith had designed to blend in with the surrounding landscape, suddenly brought everything back. I had visited her here in 1986 when I was a young journalist working at the *Age*. Judith was seventy-one, I was twenty-three. It was the only time I ever saw her in her 'natural' habitat.

Judith had greeted the photographer and me at the door, telling us she was glad we had found our way. Most people, she said, drove straight past. After a lunch of soup, bread and wine, she took us for a wander through the property. As we walked, she named the eucalypts (the peppermint gums, the white-barked brittle gums and candle gums) and talked of the animals (native rodents, wombats, kangaroos, platypuses) that she often saw on her daily rambles. She stopped by one particular gum and described how an insect had created the scribbles in the bark that look like a primitive-form of writing, while tracing the pattern with her finger. She talked of how she still loved watching birds but, with her hearing failing, she had to spin around and around before she could find them. I remembered how, intermittently, her hearing-aid would squeal with feedback.

Her final collection of poetry, *Phantom Dwelling*, had come out the year before. Many of the poems in this collection were inspired by her life in this austere, granite-strewn landscape of wind-blasted, ghostly eucalypts and low bronze heath, the ground pockmarked with abandoned goldmines. The poems are spare and concentrated, like the bush itself. There was one in particular that I liked, a meditation on how time grinds down both the landscape and the human body:

Blood slows, thickens, silts—yet when I saw you
once again, what a joy set this pulse jumping.

I had been corresponding with her for six years by the time I visited her here at Edge but I knew little of her private life. What I did know was that she had spent twenty happy years with Jack on Tamborine Mountain. I assumed that she was now living alone, and imagined that the 'you' she addressed in the poem was a vision or recollection of Jack, or a visitation in a dream. Being young and presumptuous, I saw her celebration of desire as a moving gesture of defiance, a refusal to submit to the clichés of sexless old age.

Back in Melbourne, I wrote an article for the *Age* about our day together. It ran under the headline 'Eve Alone in Her Garden', a reference to a series of poems Judith had written in which Eve addresses Adam about the mess the human race has made of this 'green world that dies'. But, of course, Eve wasn't alone in her garden. The portrait I had drawn of her—as a self-sufficient, independent, older woman serenely communing with the natural world while battling with the man-made world—was an idealised one based on partial knowledge and a desire to turn her into what I wanted her to be: an Eve who has no need of an Adam. A reflection, no doubt, of my own emotional state at the time. If I had listened more carefully, I might have noticed that, when we first arrived, she had mentioned how there were nine other households living on Half Moon. As if warning against any assumptions I might make, she added: 'It looks much more unoccupied than it is. Most of us hide in the bushes, but we call on each other for help and refuge.'

Although Nugget kept his flat at University House, he too loved Edge and regularly spent time here each week. Judith's letters to Meredith report on their daily walks through the bush. In one letter, she described how they wandered right down the boundary fence to the river, which was flooded, and found a recently killed skeleton of a kangaroo. Judith feared it had been shot. The walk inspired her poem 'River Bend' which ponders the traces of extinction and loss that linger on in this spot: the death of the kangaroo doe, whose skeleton has been cleaned 'white as moonlight', and the passing of the Aboriginal people who had once lived here. Like many of the poems in *Phantom Dwelling*, it reflected the shift that had been taking place in her poetic treatment of the landscape and her relationship with it. She was wary now of imposing meanings on to what she saw. Adopting the perspective of an indigenous tracker, she was more interested in following the clues the land threw up; learning *from* it rather than trying to remake it through language. Contemplating the kangaroo skeleton, she writes: 'Pad-tracks in sand where something drank fresh blood.'

And, more than ever before, she was immersing herself in the landscape. In the warmer months, she and Nugget would go swimming naked in the long pool between tiny rapids in the river, and picnic on its banks. The first summer at Edge, before the house was built, they camped with Meredith by the river and swam at dawn and dusk with platypuses who seemed remarkably unfazed by their presence. At night, they studied the night sky, marvelling that the stars felt close enough to throw sticks at. When Nugget was away, Judith would write to him about what was happening with the building of the house, and how she and her neighbours were banding together to oppose new goldmining applications. She would tell him about the wildlife she'd seen, which orchids were in flower, how the landscape glittered with frost and how the vegetable garden was going.

Once I learned of Judith's relationship with Nugget, I began to realise how many of the poems in *Phantom Dwelling* are indirectly addressed to him or, in a veiled way, about their relationship. While knowledge of this is not necessary to make sense of the poems, it does cast them in a new and moving light. That Edge became a bush hideaway for the clandestine lovers is beautifully captured in 'Violet Stick-insects' which zooms in on a 'landscape of leaves'. What appear to be a leaning twig and a gnawed thin-bellied leaf turn out to be two well-camouflaged stick insects, pointedly referred to as 'he and she':

> Any shadow might be a beak,
> but as twig or leaf they are safe.
> Yet he planes on a downward swing
> unfolding a brilliant wing—
> a fearless violet flash
> to centre that grey and green.

'Winter' sees them sitting around an open fire drinking red wine and contemplating old age and the paths that brought them—'you and me'—to this point. Everything—knowledge, wine, poetry, conversation, the human body—is contemplated in terms of the flow of energy which must eventually exhaust itself. There is a mood of acceptance and quiet celebration of the moment. So too in 'Late Meeting', which is, ostensibly, about the last journey a 'wind-worn bee' makes to the very last flower of autumn. This final fling between bee and flower is clearly an allegory for the coming together of Judith and Nugget.

> They meet, they mingle,
> tossed by the chilly air
> in the old ecstasy,

as though
nothing existed past
the moment's joining.

In one of her poems—published not long after Judith and Nugget became lovers—Eve addresses Adam. While the poem is not necessarily about their relationship, there are tantalising echoes of it:

Lover, we've made, between us,
one hell of a world. And yet—
still at your touch I melt. How can there be
any way out of this?
As always, I go overboard for you,
here at the world's last edge.
Ravage us still; the very last green's our kiss.

SIXTEEN

Phantom Dwelling

A child's plastic tractor lay on the dirt near the house. This time, a little boy ran out to greet us. Edge was now owned by an ex-politician from the ACT parliament, and inhabited by his niece and her family. After Judith bought Edge, she and Nugget had hatched a plan to hand it over to the Australian National University for ecological research purposes once they were too old to live there. When the handover finally happened, Judith took pleasure in the thought that it would be used to help further knowledge of the environment as a place for students to come and study. The university, however, found the cost of upkeep too onerous and later gifted the property to the Duke of Edinburgh Award Scheme to get it off their hands. While initially enthusiastic, the Scheme, which had promised to care for the land and use the buildings for youth camps, lost interest in the property and it fell into disuse.

In 2007, the Scheme decided to sell the house and land at market values. Alarmed at the way this wheeling and dealing had violated the spirit of Judith's original agreement with the university,

Meredith requested that they seek a sensitive buyer who would accept stewardship of the land, as Judith would have wished, and donate part of the proceeds to the Judith Wright Award for Indigenous Students at the Australian National University. It seemed only fair, she felt, that they offer some recompense for the huge profit they would get from selling Edge. The Scheme, however, rejected both requests.

Meredith was still saddened by the university's cavalier treatment of the property and angered by the greed of the Duke of Edinburgh Scheme, but she was glad to see the place being looked after and lived in. And it was good to know that she was always welcome to visit. We had a quick a look around, before heading down to the river for a swim. What I remembered most vividly from my first visit was the Japanese-style glass corridor that connected the living area with the bedrooms and provided views of the bush on either side. At the end of the hallway, the new inhabitants had hung a framed copy of Judith's poem 'Glass Corridor', a wry meditation on self perception inspired by the experience of walking up this passageway and seeing her reflection in the windows: 'We three walk through / a forest of tree-branches, / a swaying maze of gestures.' With moonrise on one hand and sunset on the other, the poet is left puzzling over the many selves that constitute a single human being.

This Buddhist sense of the fragmented, multitudinous self had long been with Judith. As her reputation began to grow and take on a life of its own after the publication of the acclaimed early collections, *The Moving Image* (1946) and *Woman to Man* (1949), Judith had grown uncomfortable with the public persona that went with 'being a Poet'. Behind this attitude was not just a desire for privacy and a dislike of posturing, but a recognition of the folly of clinging to a fixed identity. 'I've come more and more to think that "I" is a process, not an absolute. Once you begin to think that "I" is really real, you start trying to protect it and coddle it and bash the other person with it.' Although she never called herself a Buddhist, she shared many of its precepts and saw Buddhism as a way of learning self-control which, paradoxically, allowed one to 'do away with the self'—the isolated ego—and become one with the world, 'without argument or differences'.

This philosophy reached its fullest expression in her final poems and in the way she lived at Edge. The phrase 'phantom dwelling' comes from a letter by the seventeenth-century Japanese poet, Basho, in which he described the derelict, overgrown shack he had been living in on the shore of Lake Biwa, east of Kyoto in Japan. It was called the Hut of the Phantom Dwelling. Like Thoreau at Walden Pond or Jung in his tower by the lake, he spent his days there meditating on the changes in the seasons and the natural world. He reflected on his life and how he had once envied those in government or with impressive jobs, and how he had considered becoming a Buddhist monk. But, instead, he had spent his time writing poetry and taking journeys as aimless as the wind and clouds, while pouring out his feelings on flowers and birds. What he had achieved, he said, could never compare with the achievements of truly great writers. 'And yet we all in the end live, do we not, in a phantom dwelling?'

The 'phantom dwelling' is the web of illusions we are trapped in—a state of mind distracted by cravings and fixed ways of seeing ourselves and the world which blind us to the reality of the present moment. Judith quoted Basho's rhetorical question in her late poem 'Dust' and underscored the sentiment by naming the collection *Phantom Dwelling*. In doing so, she drew attention to her desire to strip away these illusions and live as clear-sightedly as possible; to apply what Buddhists call 'bare attention', the capacity to let go of petty obsessions and attend to the world as it is. The way she observed nature signalled how her perspective had changed. She would spend hours just watching, sometimes getting down at ground level to study the life on a patch of earth from an insect's eye view.

In 'Backyard' she describes a square of grass as a 'forest level with my eye / where travellers toil and hurry' and concentrates on 'trying to live there too'. On this small piece of ground, she uncovers whole worlds normally overlooked. All is furious activity as various creatures prepare for winter, obeying their genetic programming, their 'ancient orders', which ensure that every scrap of nutrient and energy is used and recycled. This was how she was now trying to live in her ecologically attuned house and bush property, alert to these 'ancient orders'. 'I dote on it quite amazingly,' she told a friend, 'though no doubt to most eyes it's just an untidy lot of gum trees.'

Just as the spare, pared-back, semi-arid environment of Edge changed the way she saw and appreciated nature, so too did it pare back her writing. She turned away from her traditional influences—Romantic poets like Keats and Blake—and embraced haiku 'for its honed brevities / its inclusive silences.' In that first letter she wrote to me in 1980, she had suggested that I study Chinese and Japanese poetry for their 'sterner aesthetic'. It did one good, she said, to 'pare down words to essentials and to see things clearly.' From a broader, philosophical perspective, she felt that Buddhism, with its emphasis on unity and the interconnectedness of all life on the path to Nirvana, was the kind of 'ecological ethic' the West urgently needed to adopt.

The other major influence on her during this period was, of course, the indigenous attitude to the land. Judith had always been wary of appropriating Aboriginal ideas, motifs or beliefs, and never claimed that her relationship with the natural world had the depth and comprehensiveness of the first inhabitants'. She felt, however, that non-Aboriginal Australians had much to learn from Aborigines for whom 'every part of the country . . . every mark and feature [is] numinous with meaning.' The Western notion of landscape is a limited one because it presumes a division between ourselves and the land, not to mention the rest of the cosmos. Much as she had tried to foster recognition of the deep connections between our psychic life and the phenomena of the natural world, she feared that, in the West, we would never know real kinship with the mountains, stars, moon, sun, trees and animals as our ancient forebears had.

Implicit in this fear was the recognition that, as the inheritors of Descartes' definition of humans as isolated egos in a world of lifeless matter in motion, we have lost touch with the idea of a 'living earth'. In formulating his famous maxim 'I think, therefore I am', Descartes saw the modern mind as 'solitary, autonomous and a world unto itself, unaffected by outside influence, and separate from all other beings.' Previous thinkers and theologians, who had understood God as unknowable—beyond thought and words—regarded the earth as infused with the divine and therefore alive. Such a view ensured reverence and respect for nature, says philosopher, Clive Hamilton, who has analysed the shift in Western thought underpinning the current climate crisis. Descartes' quest for certainty lead him to conceive of the cosmos as a machine—set in motion by an all-powerful God—that ran on mathematical principles. The natural world was no longer a source of wonder but a mechanism to be comprehended: spirit and matter were split asunder. This worldview was taken up by 'powerful social and political forces who wanted to sweep away any spiritual obstacles to the exploitation of the earth,' says Hamilton, paving the way for the Industrial Revolution. In belated response, environmentalism not only aims to protect and preserve nature but also seeks to bring about a return to the notion of the living earth. To remind people that 'we are dependent on the natural world, not only physically in an ecological sense, but also in some deeper, spiritual way.'

When we damage the earth, says Hamilton, we also damage ourselves.

As we left the house, we passed the few remnants of Judith's garden—some rosemary bushes, thyme, lavender, some native grasses. Outside Judith's old bedroom window is some native jasmine from a cutting from Dalwood, her great, great grandparents' house in the Hunter Valley, and which also grows at Meredith's property, Yuen. When Judith first arrived at Edge, she still longed to cultivate a garden, even if a very minimal one. She planted herbs, ferns, native plants, and started a vegetable garden. She recognised that, in conventional terms, the land was considered poor. It was rocky, with little top soil, and had been stripped and poisoned by goldmining. As always, she kept up a running commentary about her garden in her letters, although now she was not struggling against the furious rate of growth—as she had in Queensland—but against frost, drought and native animals which came to graze. She planted nettles amongst the vegetables to keep the kangaroos away and, early on, reported that she had 'a fine crop of broad beans and some nice parsley coming on, if nothing much else.'

But the land and the weather soon taught her the futility of imposing one's will upon the landscape rather than accepting it for what it is. Letting go of this impulse meant relinquishing deeply ingrained ways of relating to the land that went back to childhood. In cultivating that little garden of wild violets when her mother was ill, she had sought to work a kind of healing magic. Although this magic had failed and her mother had died, gardening had remained for Judith an expression of that longing to heal and nurture. One of the reasons she had been attracted to Edge was because it was such a visibly wounded landscape. But now she was beginning to recognise that the land would heal itself. It did not need her to tend it. Nor did it need her nostalgia for how it once was, for some dream of Eden or the 'lost garden' of her childhood.

This place's quality is not its former nature
but a struggle to heal itself after many wounds.

The compensation for relinquishing this impulse was that, now, the whole of Edge could be her garden.

Meredith led the way, looking for signs of the old paths she and her mother once followed. The land used to be more open but, in the years since Judith had lived here, a scrubby, waist-high bush called bitter pea had filled in the gaps. The way everything had become overgrown disconcerted Meredith. She stopped for a moment, trying to get her bearings. 'It's lucky we die,' she sighed, 'because everything changes and it would break your heart if you had to live through it.'

We bush-bashed our way up to the ridge, which was Judith's favourite place to watch the sun set over the Great Dividing Range. It is a low plateau of scattered quartz and iron stone boulders covered with dwarf casuarina, a kind of heath that changes colour according to the seasons. Judith knew every corner of Edge and was keenly aware of the constant changes it underwent. She developed an eye for its smallest details. During one of her walks, she discovered a rose-coloured boronia she had never seen before. With some difficulty, the botanists at the Canberra Botanical Gardens identified it as an Ice Age relic that grew only on rocky summits in this region and in Tasmania. The more she walked and looked, the keener her eye became.

Judith would send letters to Meredith telling of her 'serenely ecstatic walks' and nocturnal rambles through this rugged landscape. One recalls an 'end-of-summer evening all buzzing with beetles and rushing with ants and birds and things, everything deeply coloured and nearly autumnish, mountains violet again. Brought back the usual clutch of stones and flowers.' Meredith had given her mother a microscope which Judith would use to examine whatever she had collected.

On the way down to the river, occasional pieces of faded orange plastic ribbon tied to branches signalled that we had reconnected with the old path. We passed through what used to be a swamp, now completely dry and, further on, a large dead wattle which marked the spot where Judith, Nugget and Meredith used to camp. Through the tea-tree and ribbon gum, I could see the waterhole that Judith so loved. As she sweated her way through February heatwaves, with the sky so close she felt surrounded by blazing blue, a swim in the Mongarlowe was something she looked forward to all day.

It was a muggy morning and I was glad we had our bathers with us. Although I didn't like to admit it, even if it had been cooler I probably would have gone in, just to experience what Judith had known here. I had constantly told myself during this journey through her landscapes that I wasn't on a pilgrimage, that I hadn't come to worship—only to learn. But the distinction was a fine, and possibly arbitrary, one. Immersion in water carried with it connotations of baptism, and yet the kind of immersion I was after was more sensual than religious. I might never be able to see and know this place as Judith had, but at least I could taste some of its pleasures and, in doing so, ease my way deeper into the poems themselves.

The water was the colour of black tea. On its smooth surface, white gum blossom shimmered like tiny sequins. Because the level was lower than usual, there was very little current. Meredith warned me to watch out for rocks beneath the surface as I swam. I glided through the water, thrilled by its silky softness, stroking lazily up-river. Rolling on to my back, I watched the tall eucalypts, shaggy with bark, drift by. I don't remember the sound of birds, just the soothing rustle of water falling over the rocks at either end of the swimming hole, what Judith called a 'sunken song'. After all the travel and constant movement through the landscapes in which Judith had lived, after all the thinking and investigating and note-taking, it was good to stop. To simply float, suspended in time. This surrender, this attentiveness to the textures and sensations that make up the fabric of every instant, was the state of being her writing aspired to. Here, for a fleeting moment, I felt that I was finally inside one of her poems.

Then, of course, life intervened.

I went to stand up and struck my foot on one of those submerged rocks. Yet even this had a poetic justice to it. I remembered that Judith had written of a similar experience in one of her poems. Drought had 'stopped the song of the river' and the swimming hole had dropped so low that she bruised her knees on the rocks. It was daybreak and, as she swam, she looked at the moon, blurred by a gauze of summer dust, and recalled her mother's face looking through a grey motor-veil. Being was infused with memory, there was no escaping it:

Poems written in age confuse the years.
We all live, said Bashō, in a phantom dwelling.

This concept of life as a phantom dwelling was made all the more real for Judith by the signs of the land's previous occupants. What had once been miners' huts were now 'a tumble of chimney-stones' and old shafts near the river now sheltered 'a city of wombats'. It disturbed her that, over a hundred years after the mining was done, the remaining mullock heaps were still bare and ugly and possibly contaminated by the mercury which miners used to separate the ore. There were also old water-races used by the goldminers, and shafts sometimes five or six feet deep and hidden now by fern, tea-tree and rushes. Judith nearly fell into one the first time she stumbled across it. The fact that she didn't fall into any of these shafts or injure herself when she was on her nocturnal rambles indicates how well she grew to know this plot of earth.

Conscious as she was of the Yuin people who had first lived here, it was still hard to find traces of them. When she stood on the ridge and looked east toward the v-shaped gap between Mount Budawang and Mount Currockbilly, she knew that there had once been an Aboriginal track that ran from the Clyde River to the land around Mongarlowe and Braidwood. She knew that along these tracks to and from the coast were some bora rings, spear-sharpening grooved rocks and some scattered stone tools. Along with a couple of middens of mussel shells on the banks of the Mongarlowe, these traces were all that remained of the Yuin 'who saw the first cruel ghost-people arrive in the 1820s and lived to regret the sight.' The country remained haunted for Judith. 'This is not my land—nor anyone's; greed and the passion for ownership had done it endless damage. But I stop to look, as I scramble over the gullies and past the shafts, at the clumps of flowering wild purple Patersonia irises which it has drawn over its wounds. And the sound of the river goes on.'

As I dried myself on the riverbank, I thought of Nellie, whose story Judith tells in her poem 'River Bend'. Nellie was the last of her tribe, who, having lost her husband and children and taken to the grog to drown her sorrows, was eventually banished from the township of Braidwood. It was said that she spent her last days camped by the Mongarlowe River foraging for mussels in what must have been, it seemed to Judith, a state of 'loneliness unbearable to think of' because Aboriginal people 'live through their kind and their land'. She could still hear the woman's grief in the sound of the swollen river, 'a wild perpetual voice'.

On the way back to the house, we passed a large upright slab of granite that loomed suddenly over the track, the remains of some ancient cliff face. This rock had been special to Judith, Meredith said, because she believed it held great significance for the Yuin people. They knew, much better than we, the 'ancestral powers of stone'. When she walked this way at night, her torch would light up 'something massive, motionless' that confronted her with a sense of the numinous. In a perfect summary of the philosophy that underpinned her time at Edge, she wrote:

> I've no wish to chisel things into new shapes.
> The remnant of a mountain has its own meaning.

SEVENTEEN

Years of Love and Work

The next day, Meredith drove me back to Canberra as she, too, had work to do at the library. When we reached the outskirts, she mentioned she had recently heard about two new, adjacent suburbs that were to be named Coombs and Wright in recognition of their contribution to the city. It was one of those civic-minded public decisions that serendipitously contained a hidden story.

We went via the university so that I could revisit University House, where Judith and Nugget had spent so much time together. In one of her early letters to Nugget when he was interstate, Judith told him how she had lunched with a friend in the Fellow's Garden at University House but didn't like being there when he was away: 'Tried not to look at your windows.' As we paused by the entrance, I thought of the ploughman's lunch Judith and I had shared at the University House cafeteria in 1983. I had written asking if I could interview her for a small literary magazine for young writers I was co-editing. She replied that I could contact her on the phone number of the Aboriginal Treaty Committee office during the day. She didn't know what her evening phone number would be, as she'd be 'staying with various friends and occasionally at University House.' This, I now realised, was a reference to Nugget's flat. As always, she was carefully off-hand about the connection.

This was during the final days of the Aboriginal Treaty Committee, a voluntary organisation formed in 1979 by Judith, Nugget and a diverse group of scholars who believed that an internationally recognised treaty was the best way of achieving Aboriginal land rights. The committee advocated exclusive Commonwealth responsibility for all Aboriginal matters and for the legal recognition of the right to self-determination. It also became a mouthpiece for the public mood for change in black–white relations. Work on the treaty had consumed much of her and Nugget's time and energy for the past four years, and would culminate in Judith's book, *We Call for A Treaty* (1985), which documented their efforts and their vision for the future.

Two years before my visit, her epic account of frontier history, *The Cry for the Dead* (1981), which exposes the devastating impact on the Aborigines of 'the great pastoralist invasions of inland Australia', had been released. But I knew nothing of it when I went to talk to her that day. As well as revealing the gaps in my knowledge of her life and work, my ignorance also reflected the book's general reception. Although well reviewed, it did not have the impact she had hoped for. The general public, it seems, was not yet ready to confront the full truth about frontier history: stories of massacres and Aboriginal resistance had never been part of the 'official' story most Australians grew up with. Consequently, the book did not sell well and ended up on bookshop remainders tables. Once again, she was too far ahead of her time.

Judith and Nugget's commitment to redressing the injustices done to the indigenous people shaped every aspect of their relationship and took them far from Edge. In the late 1970s, freed from his role as political adviser, Nugget had begun to spend more time in the Northern Territory with Aboriginal communities. As Chancellor of the Australian National University, he had helped establish the university's North Australian Research Unit (NARU) in Darwin for the study of Aboriginal culture and relations between indigenous peoples and the government. NARU provided him with a base from which to work. Occasionally, Judith would join him up north.

After her first visit, she told him: 'I have washed the desert out of my hair, at last, but remember it fondly. It was a very good introduction to the country, thank you, my love.' As always, she was conscious that they might be recognised but enjoyed the excitement of an 'illicit' affair. In 1978, discussing a rendezvous in Alice Springs, she found their plans 'very alluring . . .' With uncharacteristic girlishness she wrote: 'I don't doubt our movements will be charted, out there where nothing that moves is unnoticed, but that can't be helped! I expect I ought to book into a motel for decency's sake but won't anyway—we shall see what happens. What fun!'

The need for secrecy and the possibility of being watched had a dark side for Judith, though; a dark side I had unwittingly glimpsed when she wrote to me in 1989, asking me to pass on a letter to Phillip Toyne, who was then head of the Conservation Foundation. Years of pitting herself against the deeply conservative Queensland government had made her acutely sensitive to the potential repercussions of challenging powerful vested interests. When she was campaigning to save the Barrier Reef in the 1960s, she had become convinced that she and other activists were being investigated by the CIA. The experience inspired her poem 'They':

> They look like people
> that's the trouble . . .

Only afterwards
when you're alone
you realize what you said
what the bargain was

you hear the click
as they say well thanks so much
and go off
to file the evidence.

Judith *was* the subject of an ASIO file from 1954 to 1969. ASIO's primary interest appears to have been her association with organisations regarded as communist fronts (such as the Fellowship of Australian Writers) or with people thought to be communists. While there is no evidence that the security service was interested in her environmental activism, any connection she might have had with Soviet-linked organisations could have been used to discredit her.

This experience predisposed Judith to a conspiratorial mentality, which was only heightened by her secret relationship with Nugget and the perceived sensitivity of their work for Aboriginal land rights. By 1988, she was advising Nugget to tear up her letters after reading them. As they both became heavily involved in the behind-the-scenes negotiations that led up to the *Mabo* case—which did potentially threaten powerful land holders and mining interests—her fear of surveillance escalated.

The more her hearing deteriorated—she went completely deaf in 1992—the more these anxieties preyed on her. Severe tinnitus (which involved hearing voices) and failing eyesight contributed to her feelings of isolation and vulnerability. Since the late 1980s, Nugget had been spending half the year in the Northern Territory because he was prone to life-threatening bouts of pneumonia during the colder months. Although Judith supported him in this—she knew all too well how freezing Canberra winters could be—she found his absences hard: 'It seems like years, not five months, since you left, and will be longer still.'

During this deeply troubled period, Judith destroyed two decades worth of Nugget's letters to her out of fear that they would fall into the wrong hands. On a melancholy winter's day, she burnt them in her wood fire stove.

Well, my love,

. . . it is a dreadful thing to have done but I see no alternative after weeks of thinking. Simply, there is nowhere they couldn't be found and probably nowhere that somebody wouldn't suffer for it. Forgive me for the holocaust of such a beautiful record . . . of years of love and work. Those letters were a joy to get, a personal window on your work . . . Whatever we've lost it isn't possible to lose the story-line now, and we've worked together long enough to be remembered for that.

Yours and always,

J.

Nugget was devastated. It was beyond him to destroy anything she had written to him. He brooded about Judith's isolation and felt guilty about not being with her. A year later, Judith was able to recall that 'fierce time' as a period of delusion marked by an 'inexplicable sense of bitter enemies lurking nearby.' Even thinking about it made her shake 'like a terrified horse'.

Fortunately, she stopped destroying Nugget's letters in late 1992. By this time, she had moved back to Braidwood town because she felt unable to cope with being alone at Edge. She did, however, return there when she could: 'I miss Edge severely here in this colonial village of parks and gardens, all English and tidy,' she told a friend. Nugget was relieved that she was sounding like her old self again. 'I am glad

[your] sense of being watched and intruded on is at last fading and that you can revisit Edge without trauma. It makes your distance from me more bearable.' He told her that he feared his expressions of devotion and dependence might 'sound stale with repetition and remoteness, but believe me they come from a living source.' Their correspondence went on as before, sharing news of their daily lives, their health problems, the latest football results and their work.

Even into his late eighties and early nineties, Nugget was still visiting Aboriginal communities, writing papers and flying interstate to attend functions and visit his family—as well as spending time with Judith. When his doctor told him his blood pressure was dangerously high, he complained to Judith that he couldn't start swallowing pills 'simply because I cannot finish something I am trying to write or because I wake at 2 am and brood over the state of the world.' He worried whether he would have the stamina to continue 'doing what I am lucky to have the chance to do.' In what reads hauntingly like a premonition of what was to come, he added that his real worry was 'the danger of dying of boredom being denied that chance.'

In August 1994, Judith and Nugget had one last holiday together in the Northern Territory. They used to say that they would like to end their lives by setting off into the desert together and not coming back. When they went to Ubirr Rock at Kakadu, Judith decided against going up to see the cave paintings because the spirit of the place was too powerful. She stayed at the bottom while Nugget and Meredith went on. When they returned, Judith was gone. Following a circular path, they decided to go in opposite directions to search for her on the understanding that the first to find her would return to wait at the seat. Meredith followed the path until it brought her back to the seat: neither her mother nor Nugget was there. 'The buggers,' she thought, remembering their vow. 'They've gone and done it.'

She soon found them not far away, sitting together in a little cul-de-sac. But there had been a wonderful moment of jubilation when she thought, 'Yes! Go!'

From now on, they would meet up at Edge or in Canberra. In January 1995, Nugget wrote: 'Thank you my lovely woman for those days at Edge. They were balm to my troubled spirit and a joy to my body and mind. I love you.'

Eight months later, he suffered a stroke that put him in a nursing home in Sydney and robbed him of his speech. Judith faxed him every week and visited him when she could, although travel was not easy because of her increasingly fragile health. In a letter to a friend, she wrote: 'I don't think he is in physical misery but his mind is only partly with the world . . . I don't often cry but it's hard to avoid; he wants to get out and last time I was there he thought we had come to take him [home].'

When he died in October 1997, Nugget was farewelled with a state funeral. As their relationship had never been made public, Judith was not invited. Instead, with friends and colleagues of Nugget, she held a private wake with 'good tales and memories . . . with red wine and tears and laughter.' She was relieved that he was no longer captive in his body as he had been for the previous two years. For all her sorrow, Judith's sense of his release was stronger than her feelings of loss.

In the 1950s, she had written a sonnet called 'Landscapes'. As must have happened to her many times, the poem suddenly took on a new life and meaning:

> To look at landscapes loved by the newly dead
> is to move into the dark and out again.
> Every brilliant leaf that lives by light
> dies from its hold at last and desires earth's bed:

men and trees and grasses daily falling
make that veil of beauty for her. Slight
aeons of soil on rock, of grass on soil, of men
standing on grass, can't hide her outcrops . . .
And now the newly dead
is lowered there. Now we weep for eyes whose look
is closed on landscapes loved, and at last known.

By now, Judith was living in the bed-sit in Canberra where I visited her the last time I saw her. For all the English trees and parks of Braidwood, at least there she had been out in the countryside and near Edge. Now, she was in the midst of the suburbs.

In the Canberra Botanical Gardens, shadows were stretching across the path where we sat. I was aware that Judith would be getting tired and would probably want to go, so we headed for the entrance to wait for a taxi. Judith eased herself down on to the seat of her walking frame.

'Would you like to sit on my knee?' she asked. 'This is a very strong little creature.'

'I'm fine,' I smiled, touched by her motherliness.

I wondered how she felt about going back to her bed-sit. It must have been incredibly hard, I said, moving to Canberra after so many years in the bush.

'It almost broke my heart.'

But she was near friends and medical care. And her situation was not as grim as it first appeared. She was still writing, working mostly on her autobiography. She was still involved, if less actively, in numerous causes. She still occasionally spoke out in public and on television, despite her deafness. She still regularly spent time out at Yuen with Meredith and took great pleasure in the 'garden of serenity' there. If I wanted a lesson on how to keep living well and fully into old age, she offered a fine example.

I still hadn't broached that question about death I had been wanting, all day, to ask. Worried the taxi would arrive before I got the chance, I pulled out the sheet of paper I had typed my questions on and pointed to number twenty-four, the last on the list. Judith looked at it and then at me, her eyes owl-like behind the big, round frames of her glasses.

'It doesn't frighten me,' she said. 'Be a relief.'

I should have known she would say something like this. She might write poems of naked intensity and passion, but she was not about to lay her soul bare for me or anyone else on this perfect, late summer day. If I wanted answers from her, I would have to look to her work and her example. I would have to find my own way into her 'blood's country'.

> . . . Change is my true condition,
> to take and give and promise,
> to fight and fail and alter.
>
> I aim towards Forever,
> but that is no one's country,
> till in perhaps one moment,
> dying, I'll recognise it;
>
> those peaks not ice but sunlit
> from sources past my knowing,
> its beauty of completion
> the end of being human.
>
> Judith Wright, 'Some Words'

ENDNOTES

INTRODUCTION

p. 1 This final meeting was published in the *Age*, Saturday, 21 February 1998.

p. 4 Quote 'While I'm in my five senses . . .' from 'Five Senses', Judith Wright: *Collected Poems (CP) 1942–1985*, Angus & Robertson, 1994, p. 186.

p. 7 Quote '[O]ver years past . . .', p. 334, *With Love and Fury (WLF)*, P. Clarke and M. McKinney (eds), National Library of Australia, 2006.

p. 14 Quote 'stopped the song of the river' from 'Dust', *CP*, p. 424.

p. 14 Quote 'Where is the life we have lost in living?', T. S. Eliot, Choruses from *The Rock*, Faber & Faber, 1934.

p. 16 Juvenile Poetry Notebooks, Papers of Judith Wright, MS 5781, National Library of Australia (NLA).

p. 17 Quote 'Have they dared to trample . . .' from 'The Battle', Juvenile Poetry Notebooks, Papers of Judith Wright, MS 5781, NLA.

p. 17 Quote 'green sap run . . .' from 'Never', Juvenile Poetry Notebooks, Papers of Judith Wright, MS 5781, NLA.

p. 17 Quote 'I know her . . .' from 'Wedding Photograph, 1913', *CP*, pp. 326–7.

p. 18 Quote 'since through you I lived' from 'Lovesong in Absence', *CP*, pp. 261–2.

p. 18 'The Vision', Judith Wright, *CP*, p. 262. See also *Flame and Shadow*, Shirley Walker, UQP, 1991, p. 138–9.

p. 18 Quote 'like the wood on the fire . . .' from 'Winter', *CP*, p. 425.

PART ONE—NEW ENGLAND

TRAIN JOURNEY

p. 21 Quote 'High delicate outline . . .' from 'South of My Days,' *CP*, p. 20.

p. 22 For more on John Oxley's perspective and the geology of New England see *High Lean Country: Land, People and Memory in New England*, A. Atkinson, J. S. Ryan, I. Davidson and A. Piper (eds), Allen & Unwin, 2006, pp. 23–34.

p. 22 Quote 'Harsh scarp of the tableland' from 'Nigger's Leap, New England', *CP*, pp. 15–16.

p. 23 Quote from JW's letter to John Shilliday, *WLF*, p. 334.

p. 24 JW's letter to Meredith McKinney, 29 September, 1980 and 18 November, 1980, Papers of Judith Wright, MS 5781, NLA.

p. 24 Quote 'They may have given up . . .' from *Half a Lifetime*, *(HL)*, Judith Wright, Text Publishing, p. 296.

p. 24 Quote 'small trees on their uncoloured slope' from 'Train Journey', *CP*, p. 75.

p. 25 Quote 'When the last leaf and bird go . . .' from 'Eroded Hills', *CP*, p. 81.

p. 25 Quote 'yearning for the moment of infinity . . .' from Jennifer Strauss, *Judith Wright*, Oxford, 1995, p. 46.

JEOGLA

p. 29 Quotes from Caroline Mitchell come from our visit to Jeogla and the transcript of an interview conducted in February, 2008.

p. 31 Quote 'South of my day's circle . . .' from 'South of My Days', *CP*, p. 70.

COUNCIL ROCK

p. 33 Quote 'steel-shocked earth' from 'Dust', *CP*, pp. 23–4.

p. 34 Quote 'I know a pool . . .' from juvenile poem 'The Brook', published in the *Sydney Mail*, 21 October 1925.

p. 34 All quotes from 'like an assemblage . . .' to '. . . any right to their story' are from 'The Granite Rocks of New England', Judith Wright, *The Nature of Love*, Imprint, 1997, pp. 188–92.

p. 37 Quote 'while I lectured and commanded', *ibid.*

p. 37 Quote from Peter Wright as told by his wife Jane Wright, *South of My Days*, Veronica Brady, Angus & Robertson, 1998, p. 28.

p. 37 Quote 'Who dares challenge me?' from 'The War Song of Thor' published in *Sydney Mail*, 15 May 1929.

p. 38 Quote 'men and women experienced . . .' from *The Case For God*, Karen Armstrong, The Bodley Head, 2009, p. 169.

p. 38 Quote 'the object has, in a sense, died out of our immediate experience . . .' from essay 'The Writer and the Crisis' in *Because I was Invited (BWI)*, Judith Wright, Oxford, 1975, p. 174.

p. 39 Quote 'the source of life and language', *BWI*, pp. vii-xii.

p. 39 Quote 'melt the past, the present . . .' from 'Birds', *CP*, p. 86.

p. 39 Quote 'heavy and dull' from 'Beside the Creek', *CP*, p. 226.

p. 40 Quote 'any poem might follow my pen' from 'To Hafiz of Shiraz', *CP*, pp. 215–6.

p. 40 Quote 'the ungathered alone stays beautiful . . .' from 'Beside the Creek', *CP*, p. 226.

p. 40 Quote 'There was no way of following him . . .' from Richard Holmes, *Footsteps*, Penguin, 1985, p. 26.

p. 41 Quote 'There's a spirit in each violet . . .' from 'The Spirits of the Garden', Juvenile Poetry Notebooks, Papers of Judith Wright, MS 5781, NLA.

p. 41 Quotes from 'The Garden Ghost', Juvenile Poetry Notebooks, Papers of Judith Wright, MS 5781, NLA.

p. 42 Quote 'Silence is the rock . . .' from 'Silence', *CP*, p. 121.

THE LOST GARDEN

p. 46 For more on the financial problems of David and Richard Wright, see 'Fall of a Dynasty' by Richard Guilliat, *Good Weekend*, 15 July, 2000.

p. 46 Quote 'If I was born with a tassel . . .' from interview with FC, 1998.

p. 46 Quote 'I am glad I am not there . . .' from JW's letter to Pip and Caroline, *WLF*, p. 564.

p. 46 Quote 'Now you'll understand . . .', JW's comment to David Wright, as reported by Pip Bundred to FC in 2007.

p. 47 Quotes 'cautious politeness of bankers . . .' to 'All men grow evil with trade' from 'For a Pastoralist Family', *CP*, pp. 406–10.

p. 47 Quote 'In our childish years . . .' from *HL*, p. 67.

p. 48 Quote 'Blue early mist in the valley . . .' from 'For A Pastoralist Family', *CP*, pp. 406–10.

p. 49 Quotes from 'Our Roof', Juvenile Poetry Notebooks, Judith Wright Collection, NLA.

p. 49 Quote 'I was born into a coloured country . . .' from 'Reminiscence', *CP*, p. 329.

p. 49 Quote 'Here where I walk . . .' from 'The Moving Image', *CP*, p. 3.

p. 50 Quote 'lies like a pillow . . .' from 'The World and the Child', *CP*, p. 36–37.

p. 50 Quotes from Selma Fraiberg, *The Magic Years*, Fireside, 1996, p. ix.

p. 50 Quote 'Only through this pain . . .' from 'The World and the Child', *CP*, p. 37.

p. 51 Quote 'suck and sigh of the bellows . . .' from *South of My Days*, p. 25.

p. 51 Quote 'ready to swallow him . . .' from 'Legend', *CP*, p. 97.

p. 51 Quote 'I can remember myself a time . . .' from letter by JW to Paul Sherman, *WLF*, p. 114.

p. 52 Quote 'root out everything . . .' from *HL*, p. 175.

p. 53 Quote 'that time of my mother's illness' from *Tales of a Great Aunt*, Judith Wright, Imprint, 1998, p. 11.

p. 53 Quotes from 'The Colour of Death', *The Nature of Love*, Judith Wright, Imprint, 1997, p. 112–119.

p. 54 Quote 'Have they dared . . .' from 'The Battle', Juvenile Poetry Notebooks, Papers of Judith Wright, MS 5781, NLA.

p. 54 Quote 'the land seems in some sense . . .' from Veronica Brady's article 'Documenting a Life. Judith Wright's Biography: A Delicate Balance Between Trespass and Honour' at www.nla.gov.au/events/doclife/brady.html

p. 55 Quote 'Isn't it fun when Mummy comes . . .' from 'The Flickering Candle Light' published in *Sydney Mail*, 25 May 1927.

p. 55 Quote 'grew outside the garden fences . . .' from *HL*, p. 65.

p. 57 Quotes from 'The Bush Fire', 'Drought's End' and 'The Black Coat', Juvenile Poetry Notebooks, Papers of Judith Wright, MS 5781, NLA.

p. 57 Quote 'things that did not happen in gardens' from 'The Colour of Death' in *The Nature of Love*, Imprint, 1997, p. 119.

p. 57 Letter to JW's niece, Catherine Wright, *WLF*, p. 562.

p. 58 Quote 'Cinderella considers these verses . . .' from *Sydney Mail*, 25 May 1927, p. 48.

p. 59 Quote 'I was shamefully keeping away . . .' from *HL*, p. 89.

p. 59 Quote 'she is one of the few young writers . . .' *Sydney Mail*, 31 October 1928, p. 55.

p. 59 'Halfway', *CP*, p. 290.

p. 60 Letter to Cinderella about trip to South-West Rocks from *WLF*, p. 7.

p. 60   Letter to Cinderella about Georges Creek excursion from *WLF* p. 9.

p. 61   Quote 'your delicate dry breasts . . .' from 'Train Journey', *CP*, p. 75.

p. 61   Quote 'New England is an idea . . .' from *Judith Wright* by A. D. Hope, Oxford University Press, 1975, p. 9.

p. 61   Quote 'All the hills' gathered waters . . .' from 'For New England', *CP*, p. 22.

p. 61   Recollections of return to New England from *HL*, p. 158.

GENERATIONS OF WOMEN

p. 63   Quote 'If she had wanted her children . . .' from *HL*, p. 69

p. 64   Quote 'walking slow along her garden ways . . .' from 'The Garden', *CP*, p. 35.

p. 66   Quote 'even in death she must . . .' from *Generations of Men (GOM)*, Judith Wright, Oxford, 1982, p. 232.

p. 66   Quote 'the real story of the great pastoral invasions . . .' from *Born of the Conquerors (BOC)*, Aboriginal Studies Press, 1991, p. xi.

p. 67   Quote 'that would partly be Albert's own work . . .' from *GOM*, p. 161.

p. 68   Quote 'she is entitled to her triumph . . .' from *GOM*, p. 232.

p. 68   Quote 'Bright tree, white tree . . .' from 'May Tree', Juvenile Poetry Notebooks, Papers of Judith Wright, MS 5781, NLA.

p. 68   Quote 'the enfolding, the exulting . . .' from 'The Child', *CP*, p. 34.

p. 69   'For New England', *CP*, p. 22.

p. 69   Quote 'I remember listening to them . . .' from interview with JW in *Meanjin*, 1982, p. 334.

p. 69   Quote '[I] am the gazer and the land I stare on' from 'For New England', *CP*, p. 23.

p. 69   Quote 'the place for her was alive . . .' from *GOM*, p. 181.

p. 70   Quotes from 'Remembering an Aunt', *CP*, p. 234.

p. 70   Quote 'In reality, she is one of the most . . .' from Weeta's letter to Phillip, in the possession of Meredith McKinney.

p. 70   Quote 'He may have worried himself literally to death . . .' from *HL*, p. 63.

p. 71   May's attitude to Aborigines expressed in her memoir *Memories of Far Off Days: The Memoirs of Charlotte May Wright, 1855–1929*, Peter Wright (ed.) 1988.

p. 72   Memories of Aborigines in her childhood, *HL*, p. 33.

p. 72   Albert's experience in Queensland of Aboriginal elder, see *Memories of Far Off Days*, p. 56, and 'At Coololah', *CP*, p. 140.

p. 73   Quote 'The song is gone . . .' from 'Bora Ring', *CP*, p. 8.

p. 73 Perceptions of Aborigines as a 'dying race' from Atkinson, Ryan, Davidson & Piper, eds, *High Lean Country: Land, People and Memory in New England*, Allen & Unwin, Sydney, 2006, p. 122.

p. 73 Comments on 'Bora Ring' as 'naive' and 'sentimental' from Jennifer Strauss, *Judith Wright*, Oxford University Press, Melbourne, 1995.

p. 74 Quote 'To forgive oneself . . .' from *GOM*, p. 163.

NIGGER'S LEAP

p. 77 Quote 'sheer and limelit granite head' from 'Nigger's Leap, New England', *CP*, pp. 15–16.

p. 78 Judith's feelings for Point Lookout, *BOC*, p. 30.

p. 78 Quote 'both to the idea of . . .' from *BOC*, p. 30.

p. 78 Quote 'many logs have been cut . . .' from Phillip Wright's submission to the local council in *A History of the Establishment and Administration of New England National Park*, Howard Stanley, National Parks and Wildlife Services, Sydney, p. 8.

p. 78 Quote 'Wasted—like that log . . .' from *Range the Mountains High*, Lansdowne Press, 1962, p. 79.

p. 79 Quote 'red wounds in the soil . . .', from launch of an exhibition, typed speech about trees, Judith Wright Collection, NLA.

p. 80 Acknowledges the discovery of settler's account of Darkies Point massacre, p. 30, *BOC*.

p. 81 Account of the massacre by F. Eldershaw, *Australia As It Really Is*, Darton & Co., 1854.

p. 82 Quotes 'Each of our men was savagely anxious . . .' to 'sick of the horrid carnage below . . .' from Eldershaw, pp. 64–73.

p. 82 Quotes from 'deeply degraded beings' to 'the wasting territories . . .' from Eldershaw, pp. 88–102.

p. 83 Quote 'Night lips the harsh . . .' from 'Nigger's Leap, New England', *CP*, p. 15.

p. 83 Quote from JW 'It was no 'wilderness . . . forgiveness.', *BOC*, p. 30.

DREAMSCAPE

p. 84 JW's dream diary is in the private possession of Meredith McKinney.

p. 85 Quote 'They reveal their significance . . .', Carl Gustav Jung as quoted by E A Bennet in *What Jung Really Said*, Abacus, 2001, pp. 92–3.

p. 86 Reference to Paul Ehrlich in JW's essay 'Our Vanishing Chances', *BWI*, p. 239.

p. 86 Quote 'the juggernaut machines . . .' from 'Habitat', *CP*, pp. 297–309.

PART TWO: QUEENSLAND

THE LANDSCAPE OF LOVE

p. 93 Quote 'What I saw now in Queensland . . .' from *HL*, p. 175.

p. 93 Quote 'lost in a desolate country' from 'The Forest', a dedication, *CP*, p. 184.

p. 94 Quote 'If not, I left it across the way . . .' from *Equal Heart and Mind (EHM), Letters Between Judith Wright and Jack McKinney*, Patricia Clarke and Meredith McKinney (eds), UQP, 2004, p. 62.

p. 94 Quote 'the sweet white flesh of lilies . . .' from 'Botanical Gardens', *CP*, p. 85

p. 94 Quote 'two lovely trees in bloom . . .' from letter to Nugget Coombs, MS 802, Box 49, Folders 378–383, NLA.

p. 95 Quote 'secretly sealed with love' from *EHM*, p. 19.

p. 95 Quote 'a sharp and gentle observer' from *Southerly*, vol. 61, no.1, 2001.

p. 96 Quote 'The gift of the poet is to *feel* . . . ' from 'The Poet and the Intellectual Environment', *Meanjin*, vol. 1, no. 2, p. 47.

p. 96 Quote 'suffer not only *more* than others, but to suffer *for* others . . .' from 'The Poet and the Modern World', *Meanjin*, vol. 1, no. 3, p. 80.

p. 96 Quote 'I am a tranquil lake . . .' from 'The Maker,' *CP*, p. 30.

p. 97 For more on Jack's philosophical views, see *The Structure of Modern Thought*, J. P. McKinney, Chattos & Windus, 1971.

p. 98 Quote 'the values of feeling . . .' from *HL*, p. 208.

p. 98 Quotes from Clive Hamilton from 'The Rebirth of Nature and the Climate Crisis', A Sydney Ideas Lecture, University of Sydney, 7 July 2009 at www.clivehamilton.net.au/cms/media/documents/the_rebirth_of_nature_and_the_climate_crisis,pdf, p. 15.

p. 98 Quote 'an intellectual atom bomb' from *EHM*, p. 146.

p. 98 Quote 'the froth on the top of the cauldron . . .' from Brigid Rooney, *Literary Activists*, UQP, 2009, p. 15.

p. 98 Reviews of *The Structure of Modern Thought* published in *Philosophy and Phenomenological Research*, Vol. 34, No. 3 (Mar. 1974), pp. 449–50, and *The Philosophical Quarterly*, Vol. 22, No. 89. (Oct., 1972), pp. 365–6.

p. 99 Quote 'because you are my home' from 'Two Hundred Miles', *CP*, p. 96.

p. 99 Quote 'we are going to be very happy & defy the world' from *EHM*, p. 132.

p. 99 Quote 'we live so much on the heights . . .' from *EHM*, p. 134.

p. 100 Quote 'I think we'll live and die in separate houses . . .' *EHM*, p. 106.

p. 100 Quote 'when we are most, then we are least alone' from 'City Asleep', *CP*, p. 49.

p. 101 Quote from 'time's own root' from 'The Cycads', *CP*, p. 39.

MY RED MOUNTAIN

p. 103 Quote 'Already the last of the gravel red roads are being bitumened . . .' from *WLF*, p. 264.

p. 103 Quote 'my red mountain' from 'Two Hundred Miles, *CP*, p. 96–7.

p. 104 Quote 'the rich dark rainforest . . .' from *EHM*, p. 2.

p. 104 Quote 'More and more I feel there isn't an "I" . . .' from *WLF*, p. 265.

p. 104 Quote from 'Rainforest' from *CP*, p. 412.

p. 105 Quote 'From time immemorial, nature was always filled . . .' from Jung, *Essays on Contemporary Events*, Routledge, 2002, p. 78

p. 105 Quote 'wild long dreams involving the whole of life and death . . .' from *WLF*, p. 92.

p. 105 Quote 'being part of the galaxy . . .' from *WLF* p. 276.

p. 105 Quote 'At times I feel as if I am spread out . . .' from *Memories, Dreams, Reflections*, Carl Gustav Jung and Aniela Jaffe, Pantheon, 1973, p. 225.

p. 106 Quote from 'Sanctuary' from *CP*, p. 139.

p. 108 Quote 'a kind of hostility still . . .' from *HL*, p. 248.

p. 108 Quote from JW's dream from her dream diary in the possession of Meredith McKinney.

p. 109 Quote 'Since nobody is capable of recognising . . .' from Jung, *Essays on Contemporary Events*, Routledge, 2002, p. 93.

p. 109 Quotes from 'Camphor Laurel' from *CP*, p. 35.

IN THE DARK WOOD

p. 112 Quote from 'The Ancestors' from *CP*, p. 111.

p. 112 Quote 'Just as the body . . .' from Carl Gustav Jung, *The Basic Writings*, The Modern Library, 1993, p. 42.

p. 112 Quote 'knowing in a dreadful way . . .', *Portrait of a Friendship: The Letters of Barbara Blackman and Judith Wright 1950–2000* (*POF*), The Miegunyah Press, 2007, p. 39.

p. 113 Quote 'Those who see the Mountain today have no idea . . .', *The Turning Years*, Eve Curtis, self-published, 1990, p. 155.

p. 114 Quote 'It is only if reason can draw upon . . .' from Terry Eagleton, *Reason, Faith and Revolution*, Yale University Press, 2009, p. 110.

p. 114 Quote 'our feelings and emotions must be engaged . . .' *BWI*, p. 206.

p. 114 Quote 'not only rational recognition . . .' from *BWI*, pp. 206–7.

p. 114 Jonathan Bates, *Song of the Earth*, Picador, 2000, p. 23.

p. 115 Quote 'we must regenerate ourselves . . .' from *BWI*, p. 206.

p. 115 Quote 'Take their cold seed . . .' from 'The Cycads', *CP*, p. 39.

p. 116 Quote from 'The Forest Path', *CP*, p. 111.

p. 116 Quote 'we are beginning to recognise that we are not . . .' from *WLF*, p. 218.

p. 117 Quote 'one of the mountain's extra special days . . .', *WLF*, p. 127.

p. 117 Observation about suicides in National Parks from Raymond Curtis, interview with Fiona Capp, April 2009.

p. 117 Quotes from 'The Precipice', *CP*, pp. 120–1.

BEYOND THE BURNING WIND

p. 119 Quote 'We were fortunate, house . . .' from 'Habitat', *CP*, pp. 297–309.

p. 120 Quote 'Heraldic animals . . .' from 'Habitat', *CP*, p. 305.

p. 121 Quote 'one of the glories' from 'Rain-forests of south-eastern Queensland in Summer', *Wildlife*, vol. 1, no.1.

p. 122 Quote 'garden to wander in' from *WLF*, p. 185.

p. 123 Quote 'It rejoices me to have one now' from *WLF*, p. 116.

p. 123 Quote 'I was born into a coloured country . . .' from 'Reminiscence', *CP*, pp. 329–30.

p. 123 Quote 'full of violets, wattle, and daffodils . . .' from *POF*, p. 242

p. 123 Quote 'My childhood is divided . . .' from *HL*, p. 37.

p. 124 Quote 'I hold the crimson fruit . . .' from 'The Maker', *CP*, pp. 29–30.

p. 124 Quote 'I am the earth . . .' from 'Woman to Child', *CP*, pp. 28–9.

p. 124 Quote 'What cooks out of sight in the basement . . .' from *POF*, p. 16.

p. 124 Quote 'living earth' from *BWI*, p. vii.

p. 125 Quote 'overmastered by life' from 'The Waiting Ward', *CP*, p. 104.

p. 125 Quote 'I am the garden beyond . . .' from 'The Watcher', *CP*, p. 105.

p. 125 Reference to 'Old Woman's Song', *CP*, p. 194.

p. 126 Quote 'the garden is rather a dream', from Letter to Kathleen McArthur, 1952/3, MS 5781, Box 78, folder 568, NLA.

p. 126 Reference to the stars as the garden's flowers, 'Naming the Stars', p. 203.

p. 126 Quote 'swarm of honey bees' from 'Stars' *CP*, p. 52.

p. 126 Quote 'Darkness where I find my sight', 'Midnight', *CP*, p. 59.

p. 127 Reference to lying in the garden and looking at the stars, *WLF* p. 203 & *POF*, p. 221.

p. 127 Quote 'neon night . . .' from 'Western Star', *CP*, p. 123.

p. 127 Quote 'towering universe' from 'Praise for the Earth', *CP*, p. 188.

p. 127 Quote 'some sad man-wrought . . .' from 'White Night', *CP*, p. 324.

p. 127 Quote 'I've got no sense of public service whatever' from *EHM*, p. 102.

p. 128 Reference to bulldozing the countryside on an unprecedented scale, See *Patriots*, *Defending Australia's Natural Heritage*, UQP, 2006, p. 20.

p. 129 Quotes from 'That Seed', *CP*, p. 332.

p. 129 Quote 'down the creek the chain-saw . . .' from *POF*, p. 30.

EYE OF THE EARTH

p. 132 Quote 'No one has marked the sea' from 'Sea-Beach', *CP*, p. 138.

p. 132 Quote 'delectably perched on a lake shore . . .' from *HL*, p. 280.

p. 132 Quote 'wild and birdy lakes . . .' from *WLF*, p. 83.

p. 132 Quote 'All day the candid staring of the lake . . .' from 'The Lake', *CP*, p. 189.

p. 133 Quote 'blue as a doll's eye' from *WLF*, p. 109.

p. 133 Quote 'in that little, light-filled concrete house . . .' from *HL*, p. 283.

p. 134 Quote from 'Pelicans', *CP*, p. 171.

p. 134 Quote 'forest of symbols for poetic harvesting' from Jennifer Strauss, *Judith Wright*, Oxford University Press, 1995, p. 93.

p. 134 Quote 'Words are not meanings for a tree', from 'Gum-Trees Stripping', *CP*, p. 133.

p. 134 Mention of tantalising scribbles on trunk of a gum refers to 'Scribbly-Gum,' p. 131, *CP*.

p. 135 Quote 'I am a tranquil lake . . .' from 'The Maker'. *CP*, p. 29–30.

p. 135 Quote 'eye of the earth' from 'The Lake', *CP*, p. 189.

p. 135 Quote 'pool, jet-black and mirror-still' from 'Egrets', *CP*, p. 166.

p. 137 Reference to the declaration of Cooloola as a National Park from *Patriots*, William J. Lines, UQP, 2006, p. 96.

p. 137 Reference to Cooloola sandmass as largest continuous series of sand dunes in the world, and Aborigines of the region from *Wildflowering*, Margaret Somerville, UQP, 2004, p. 134 and p. 153.

p. 137 Quote 'so horizontal blue' and 'clear black like a mirror . . . all different' from *WLF*, p. 83.

p. 139 Quotes 'the certain heir of the lake' to 'white shores of sand . . .' from 'At Cooloolah' *CP*, p. 140.

p. 139 Quote 'Some things ought to be left secret . . .' from 'Lyrebirds', *CP*, p. 176.

p. 141 Big Snake story from 'For Christine', Papers of Judith Wright, MS 5781, NLA.

p. 142   Quote 'tropical gulag' from *Tall Man*, Chloe Hooper, Hamish
         Hamilton, 2008, p. 11.

p. 142   'The Graves at Mill Point' from *CP*, p. 193.

p. 143   'Lake in Spring' from *CP*, p. 333.

THE LANDSCAPE OF GRIEF

p. 145   Quote 'an obscure hamlet' and subsequent references to this journey are
         from JW's memoir about Jack's death published in *EHM*, pp. 186–190.

p. 146   Quote 'Suffer, wild country . . .' from 'Australia 1970', *CP*, pp. 287–8.

p. 147   Letter to Jack Blight about Jack's death, p. 177, *WLF*.

p. 147   JW's dreams after Jack's death from her dream diary.

p. 148   Quote 'It's so good getting back there, with the garden to dig in,' *POF*,
         p. 207.

p. 148   Quotes 'Here still, the mountain that we climbed . . .' to 'steep
         unyielding rock' from 'This Time Alone', *CP*, pp. 260–61.

p. 148   Reference to poem about being trapped beneath the earth from
         'Eurydice in Hades', *CP*, p. 264.

p. 149   Quote 'stuck at the bottom of a page as though it were a cliff edge',
         WLF, p. 131.

p. 150   Quotes 'fountain of hot joy' to 'Out of the torn earth's mouth . . .' from
         'Flame-tree in a Quarry', *CP*. p. 60.

p. 151   Quote 'great blossoming of the mountain's flame trees . . .' from
         Kathleen McArthur's tribute to Judith Wright, Papers of Judith Wright,
         MS 5781, Box 104, Folder 747, NLA.

p. 151   Quote 'this sudden season' from 'The Flame-tree', *CP*, p. 95.

p. 151   Quote 'the equal heart and mind' from 'The Forest', *CP*, p. 184.

p. 152   Quote 'Now, in its eighteenth spring . . .' from 'The Flame-tree Blooms',
         CP, p. 287.

p. 152   Quote 'Not till those fiery . . . be one' from 'All Things Conspire', *CP*, p. 93.

p. 153   Quote 'whistling one of Jack's tunes' from *POF*, p. 235.

p. 153   Quote 'rather beautiful people . . .' from *WLF*, p. 268.

p. 154   Memories of Calanthe from 'Habitat', *CP*, p. 297.

p. 154   Quote 'secret place behind the world' from 'Dialgoue', *CP*, p. 131.

p. 154   Reference to unbridgeable gulf from 'Space Between', *CP*, p. 314.

p. 154   Quote 'the garden is so huge . . .' from *POF*, p. 212.

p. 154   Quote 'the best of my life has been lived here' from *WLF*, p. 195.

p. 154   Quote 'So many places I can see . . .' from *POF*, p. 317.

p. 155   Poem about an old boat tied up on the lake from 'Half Dream',
         CP, p. 347.

p. 155   Dream from JW's dream diary in the possession of Meredith McKinney.

p. 155   Quote 'tiny, vulnerable planet . . .' from *BWI*, p. 254.

p. 155   Quote 'detached from some bond . . .' from JW's dream diary.

p. 156   Quote 'I'm tired now, summers . . .' from 'Moving South', *CP*, pp. 386–7.

p. 156   'At Cedar Creek', *CP*, p. 379.

p. 157   Quote 'Whatever Being is . . .' from 'Lament for Passenger Pigeons', *CP*, p. 319.

p. 158   Quote 'mythopoetic connection to the landscape' from *WLF*, p. 521.

p. 158   Quote 'losing the first was grief . . .' from JW's dream diary.

PART THREE: ACT & MONGARLOWE

OPERA CITY

p. 161   Quotes 'fantasy of power' and 'rhetorical opera city' from 'Brief Notes on Canberra', *CP*, pp. 351–4.

p. 162   Mention of tree outside her flat at University House from *WLF*, p. 256.

p. 162   Quotes 'no balance between . . .' and 'an ecological miracle' from 'Brief Notes on Canberra, *CP*, pp. 351–4.

p. 163   Quote 'Let love not fall from me . . .' from 'Prayer', *CP*, p. 229.

p. 164   Quote 'Indeed, it is difficult for me to identify . . .' from *Aboriginal Autonomy*, H. C. Coombs, Cambridge, 1994, p. xv.

p. 164   Quote 'Barbara Blackman wants to give me . . . long time, my love' from Papers of Nugget Coombs, MS 802, Box 49, F 378–83, NLA, letter dated 22 April, 1975.

p. 166   Quote 'it entails a whole new philosophy of living . . .' *BWI*, p. 254.

p. 167   Quote 'climate change, pollution of land and sea . . .' from 'Recollections of Nugget Coombs, Public Servant', Papers of Judith Wright, MS 5781, Box 87, Folder 625, NLA.

p. 168   Quote 'everything here is immediately . . .' from *WLF*, p. 260.

p. 168   Reference to a friend that she was a territorial animal from *WLF*, p. 256.

p. 168   Quote 'long slope that goes down . . .' from *WLF*, p. 266.

p. 169   Quote 'the land is so lovely . . .', *WLF*, p. 285.

THE WORLD'S LAST EDGE

p. 175   Quote 'blood slows . . .' from 'Pressures' *CP*, p. 424.

p. 175   Interview with JW by Fiona Capp, *The Age* 27 June, 1986.

p. 175   Quote 'this green world that dies' from 'Eve Sings', *CP*, p. 358.

p. 176 Reference to letter to Meredith about flooded river and recently killed kangaroo skeleton from JW's letter to Meredith McKinney, 5 June, 1978, Papers of Judith Wright, MS 5781, NLA.

p. 176 Quotes 'white as moonlight' and 'pad tracks in the sand . . .' from 'Riverbend, *CP*, p. 416.

p. 177 Quotes 'landscape of leaves' and 'Any shadow might be a beak . . .' from 'Violet Stick-Insects', *CP*, p. 416.

p. 177 'Winter', *CP*, p. 425.

p. 177 Quotes 'They meet, they mingle . . .' from 'Late Meeting', *CP*, pp. 399–400.

p. 178 Quote 'Lover, we've made between us . . .' from 'Eve Scolds', *CP*, pp. 359–360.

PHANTOM DWELLING

p. 180 Quote 'We three walk through . . .' from 'Glass Corridor', *CP*, p. 418.

p. 180 Quote 'I've come more and more to think . . .' from *WLF*, p. 109.

p. 181 Quote 'do away with the self' from Papers of Judith Wright, MS 5781, essay on Tinnitus, Box 104, Folder 746, NLA.

p. 181 Quote 'And yet we all in the end live . . .' from Matsuo Basho, 'The Hut of the Phantom Dwelling', *Four Huts: Asian Writings on the Simple Life*, B. Watson and S. Addiss, Shambhala, 1994, p. 85.

p. 182 Quotes 'a forest level with my eye . . .' to 'ancient orders' from 'Backyard', *CP*, pp. 397–8.

p. 182 Quote 'I dote on it quite amazingly' from pp. 344–5, *WLF*.

p. 182 Quote 'for its honed . . .' from 'Bevity' p. 413, *CP*.

p. 182 Quote 'every part of the country . . .' as quoted in Veronica Brady *South of My Days,* Angus & Robertson, 1998, p. 433.

p. 183 Reference to kinship with stars, mountains from *BOC*, p. 14.

p. 183 Quotes 'solitary, autonomous and a world unto itself . . .' and all other from Clive Hamilton, interview with Alan Saunders on 'The Philosopher's Zone', ABC Radio National, 18 July 2009. For the essay which inspired this discussion see 'The Rebirth of Nature and the Climate Crisis' by Clive Hamilton on his website.

p. 185 Quote 'this place's quality is not its former nature . . .' from Summer, *CP*, p. 421.

p. 185 Quote 'end-of-summer evening . . .' from letter dated 20 March, 1982, MS 802, Box 104, Folder 746, NLA.

p. 187 Quotes 'drought had stopped the song of the river . . .' to 'Poems written in age . . .' from 'Dust', *CP*, p. 424.

p. 187 Quote ' a city of wombats' from 'Summer', *CP*, p. 421.

p. 188 Quotes 'who saw the first cruel ghost-people arrive' to 'live through their kind and their land' from 'From Ridge To River', unpublished essay, Papers of Judith Wright, MS 5781, NLA.

p. 188 Quote 'a wild, perpetual voice' from 'Riverbend', *CP*, p. 416.

p. 189 Quotes 'the ancestral powers of stone' to 'I've no wish to chisel things . . .' from 'Rockface', *CP*, p. 420.

YEARS OF LOVE AND WORK

p. 190 Quote 'Tried not to look at your windows' from November 1976, Papers of Nugget Coombs, MS 802, Box 49, Folder 378–83, NLA.

p. 192 Quote 'I have washed the desert . . .', date unknown, Papers of Nugget Coombs, MS 802, Box 49, folder 378–83, NLA.

p. 192 Quote 'the plans sound very alluring' 25 April, 1978, Papers of Nugget Coombs, MS 802, Box 49, folder 378–83, NLA.

p. 192 Quote 'They look like people . . .' from 'They', *CP*, p. 349.

p. 193 JW's ASIO file: CRS A6119/79, M/82/108, Volume 1, Australian Archives, Canberra.

p. 194 Quote 'Well my love . . .', 18 June, 1992, Papers of Nugget Coombs, MS 802, Box 49, Folder 379, NLA.

p. 194 Quote 'I miss Edge severely . . .' from letter to Len Webb, 1 November 1992, Papers of Judith Wright, MS 5781, NLA.

p. 194 Quote 'I am glad [your] sense of being watched . . .' from letter to JW, 6 May 1993, Papers of Judith Wright, MS 5781, Box 72, Folder 514, NLA.

p. 195 Quote 'sound stale with repetition and remoteness, but believe me . . .' from letter to JW, 21 June 1994, Papers of Judith Wright, MS 5781, NLA.

p. 195 Quote 'simply because I cannot finish . . .' from letter to JW, 6 May 1993, Papers of Judith Wright, MS 5781, Box 72, Folder 514, NLA.

p. 196 Quote 'Thank you my lovely woman . . .' from letter to JW, Papers of Judith Wright, MS 5781, Box 72, NLA.

p. 196 Quote 'I don't think he is in physical misery . . .' from letter to Len Webb, 12 December 1995, Papers of Judith Wright, MS 5781, NLA.

p. 196 Quote 'good tales and memories . . .' from *WLF*, p. 544.

p. 196 Quote 'To look at landscapes loved by the newly dead . . .' from 'Landscapes', *CP*, p. 141.

SELECT BIBLIOGRAPHY

Atkinson, Ryan, Davidson & Piper, eds, *High Lean Country: Land, People and Memory in New England*, Allen & Unwin, Sydney, 2006.

Bates, Jonathan, *Song of the Earth*, Picador, London, 2000.

Blomfield, Geoffrey, *Baal Belbora: The End of the Dancing*, Alternative Publishing Cooperative, Sydney, 1985.

Brady, Veronica, *South of My Days: A Biography of Judith Wright*, Angus & Robertson, Sydney, 1998.

Coombs, H. C., *Aboriginal Autonomy*, Cambridge University Press, Cambridge, 1994.

The Return of Scarcity: Strategies for an Economic Future, Cambridge University Press, Cambridge, 1990.

Curtis, Eve, *The Turning Years*, self-published, 1990.

Eldershaw, F., *Australia As It Really Is*, Darton & Co., 1854.

Fraiburg, Selma, *The Magic Years*, Fireside, New York, 1996.

Holmes, Richard, *Footsteps*, Penguin, London, 1985.

Hope, A. D., *Judith Wright* by A. D. Hope, Oxford University Press, Melbourne, 1975.

Jung, Carl, *The Basic Writings*, The Modern Library, New York, 1993

Memories, Dreams, Reflections, Flamingo, London, 1983

Essays on Contemporary Events, Routledge, London, 2002.

Lines, William, *Patriots: Defending Australia's National Heritage*, UQP, St Lucia, 2006.

McKernan, Susan, *A Question of Commitment: Australian Literature in the Twenty Years After the War*, Allen & Unwin, Sydney, 1989.

McKinney, J. P., *The Structure of Modern Thought*, Chatto & Windus, London, 1971.

Mead, Philip, *Networked Language*, Australian Scholarly Publishing, Melbourne, 2008.

Rooney, Brigid, *Literary Activists: Writer-intellectuals and Australian Public Life*, UQP, St Lucia, 2009.

Rowse, Tim, *Nugget Coombs: A Reforming Life*, Cambridge University Press, Cambridge, 2002.

Scott, W. N. *Focus on Judith Wright*, UQP, St Lucia, 1967.

Somerville, Margaret, *Wildflowering: The Life and Places of Kathleen McArthur*, UQP, St Lucia, 2004.

Strauss, Jennifer, *Judith Wright*, Oxford University Press, Melbourne,1995.

Walker, Shirley, *Flame and Shadow: A Study of Judith Wright's Poetry*, UQP, St Lucia, 1991.

Judith Wright: Australian Bibliographies, Oxford University Press, Melbourne, 1981.

Wright, Charlotte May, *Memories of Far Off Days: The Memoirs of Charlotte May Wright, 1855–1929*, Peter Wright (ed), self-published, 1988.

Wright, Judith, *Collected Poems, 1942–85*, Angus & Robertson, Sydney, 1994.

Half a Lifetime, Text Publishing, Melbourne, 1999.

The Nature of Love, Sun Books 1966, re-printed by Imprint, Sydney, 1997.

Range the Mountains High, Judith Wright, Lansdowne Press, Melbourne, 1962.

Because I Was Invited, Oxford University Press, Melbourne, 1975.

Tales of a Great Aunt, Imprint, 1998.

Generations of Men, Oxford University Press, Melbourne, 1959.

The Coral Battleground, Thomas Nelson, Melbourne, 1977.

The Cry for the Dead, Oxford University Press, Melbourne, 1981.

We Call for a Treaty, Collins/Fontana, Sydney, 1985.

Born of the Conquerors, Aboriginal Studies Press, Canberra, 1991.

The Equal Heart & Mind: Letters Between Judith Wright & Jack McKinney, Patricia Clarke and Meredith McKinney (eds), UQP, St Lucia, 2004.

With Love and Fury: Selected Letters of Judith Wright, Clarke & McKinney, (eds), National Library of Australia, Canberra, 2006.

Portrait of a Friendship: The Letters of Barbara Blackman and Judith Wright 1950–2000, The Miegunyah Press, Melbourne, 2007.

ACKNOWLEDGMENTS

I have been so very fortunate, when researching and writing this book, to have had the support and encouragement of three exceptional Wright women—Judith's daughter, Meredith McKinney, and Judith's oldest nieces, Pip Bundred and Caroline Mitchell. I am deeply grateful to them all. *My Blood's Country* would be a very different book had it not been for their willingness to share their knowledge and experience of Judith and the Wright family, and for helping me navigate Judith's heartland.

Meredith provided me with permission to read her letters to her mother in the NLA, put me up when I visited her at 'Yuen' and was generous in her recollections of her mother and of her own experiences as Judith's daughter. She gave me access to Judith's only remaining dream diary (not previously cited in any account of Judith's life and work) and transcribed many of the dreams for me. She also provided family photographs, useful information about her father's philosophy, and invaluable advice about how to track down important places in Judith's life.

When I was researching Judith's childhood years in New England, Caroline Mitchell and her husband, John Mitchell, were wonderful hosts. Caroline not only gave me and my friend Cheryl Donohue a roof over our heads and meals during this unforgettable week, but also orchestrated our visits to Wallamumbi, Wongwibinda, Thalgarrah, Point Lookout, Jeogla and Hillgrove. She was generous in her recollections of Judith and her own memories of growing up in New England, and with books about the family.

Pip Bundred was equally generous with her memories of Judith and life in New England and with books about the family, and provided some memorable lunches at Red Hill.

Many thanks to Sally and Edward Wright for lunch at Wongwibinda and for the tour of the property, and to Geraldine Robertson for the hours she spent showing us around Thalgarrah, even though this visit did not, for thematic reasons, make it into the book.

It was a real joy to have the company of two good friends, Cheryl Donohue, during the New England part of the journey, and Anna Murdoch, in Brisbane, Mt Tamborine and Boreen Point.

For their knowledge of the history and natural history of Mt Tamborine, I am indebted to Eve and Raymond Curtis. I am also very grateful to local historians, Paul Lyons and Ron Pokarier, for guiding me through Judith's landscapes on Tamborine and for providing useful information.

While my book is neither biography nor academic analysis, it has benefited from the scholarship and insights of many fine thinkers in the field. A number of books on Judith's life and work have been particularly helpful and illuminating: Veronica Brady's biography *South of My Days*, Jennifer Strauss's analysis of Judith's poetry and activism, *Judith Wright*, and Shirley Walker's *Flame and Shadow: A Study of Judith Wright's Poetry*. Also invaluable have been the two collections of Judith's letters, *The Equal Heart and Mind: Letters Between Judith Wright and Jack McKinney*, and *With Love and Fury: Selected Letters of Judith Wright*, both of which were edited by Meredith McKinney and Patricia Clarke. It was a stroke of good fortune that the letters between Judith Wright and Nugget Coombs became available from the NLA at the beginning of 2009, while I was still researching and writing this book. There is still much to be written about this remarkable relationship.

I am also grateful to:

Nonie Sharp, who kindly shared her memories of Judith, along with her essays on Judith's writing and activism; Jean Newall, archivist, New England Girls' School for tracking down the poems of Judith's that were published in the school magazine; the librarians at the National Library of Australia for their help with the Judith Wright and Nugget Coomb papers; the librarians at *The Age* and *Sydney Morning Herald* libraries for copies of Judith's juvenile poems published in the *Sydney Mail*; and to John Shilliday, who, as Principal at Ivanhoe Girls Grammar during my time there was responsible for inviting Judith to the school.

As always, my final thanks go to my partner, Steven Carroll, and to my son, Leo Carroll-Capp.